CAMPAIGN 1996:
WHO'S WHO IN THE RACE FOR THE WHITE HOUSE

An essential election-year travel guide, for political junkies and voters alike, to the combination circus and marathon that leads to the Oval Office on November 5, 1996.

Two seasoned Washington reporters provide answers to questions such as:

- Why will the state of voters' pocketbooks be more important this November than any other issue? Answer: Shrinking paychecks frighten voters more than the Bosnia crisis.
- Why will hot-button issues such as abortion rights, gun control, and school prayer mean more to voters early in the primaries and less so in the general election? Answer: Primaries give greater weight to the radical wings of both Democratic and Republican parties; the general election sees candidates move more to the center where the bulk of the voters are.
- When will the major-party tickets finally be chosen? And when will the voters know who the final choices will be in November? Answer: Both parties can sew up their nominations as early as April; the full roster of independents may not be complete before July.
- Where is Bill Clinton likely to lose his commanding lead over most Republican rivals? And which states must he have to be reelected? Answers: The Deep South and the Northern Industrial Belt, respectively. Key State? As California goes, so goes the nation.
- How can both Republicans and Democrats win? The best bet is for a Clinton win for President and a further strengthening of the Republican hold on Congress and the fifty state legislatures and governors' mansions!
- How will *you* and the voters of your state stack up against the rest of America on Election Day 1996?

CAMPAIGN 1996:

WHO'S WHO IN THE *RACE* FOR THE WHITE HOUSE

JAMES L. SRODES
AND
ARTHUR JONES

HarperPaperbacks
A Division of HarperCollinsPublishers

HarperPaperbacks   *A Division of* HarperCollins*Publishers*
                    10 East 53rd Street, New York, N.Y. 10022

Portions of this work have previously appeared in *Financial World* magazine.

Cover photographs by Sygma

First printing: February 1996

Printed in the United States of America

HarperPaperbacks and colophon are trademarks of HarperCollins*Publishers*

❖ 10 9 8 7 6 5 4 3 2 1

TABLE OF CONTENTS

PART TWO: PLAYERS AND SPOILERS

TABLES

Who's Who in the
Race
for the
White House

INTRODUCTION

THE GENIUS OF THE FOUNDING FATHERS WAS THAT they realized their great American political experiment must continue to change indefinitely. They had the wisdom to concede that the Constitution they framed in Philadelphia in 1787 could not address, let alone solve, all the problems a great nation would face over the years. They had confidence that future generations would be able to make the adjustments necessary to keep the country on course. So the history of the political system of the United States has been one of constant tinkering, of trial and error.

On its long journey America has been confronted by numerous crossroads and has had to shift its political objectives as the times required. There have been hectic periods of mobilization for wars of survival, there have been noble experiments in social progress, and there have been fallow periods and periods of consolidation. The presidential election of 1996 brings the country to yet another turning in our journey.

This primer on the upcoming campaign sprang from our notion that there was a need not only to more fully identify the candidates in the swarm of rivals who seek the White House but also to examine more closely where we stand as a nation at this historic juncture. This crossroads is surely an important one. American voters are less and less willing to trust the two established parties to provide the real choices for how we govern ourselves. A conflicting chorus of "third party" opinions and options will produce a noise level not witnessed since the cacophony of the early Roosevelt New Deal years.

Democratic party theorists like to compare their situation today to the challenge that faced Harry S. Truman in his 1948 bid to transform the power bloc of the Roosevelt New Deal–World War II coalition to a peacetime force for progress. Republicans harken back to Ronald Reagan's election in 1980, which signaled the end of the Kennedy-Johnson mandate to create a Great Society based on social fairness. Both party establishments appear to have missed the point, though. If any similar period of change springs to mind, it must be the chaotic 1856 election, which saw the long-established coalitions of the Whig Party begin to fracture and disappear even as the Republican Party began to form around the issues of westward expansion and the abolition of slavery. The 1856 election was four years too early for the nascent Republicans to consolidate themselves behind their issues and, just as important, behind the candidate Abraham Lincoln, who would push the party into its late-nineteenth-century ascendancy. So voters compromised on the well-intentioned Democrat James Buchanan, who was powerless to divert the tides that soon swept the country into civil war.

Just as we were 140 years ago, America is standing at another turning point, one where the policies and alignments of the past no longer serve us as well as they once did. Yet we have not decided on the mix of governance— the balance between Washington and the states, the political choices of who does what for whom—that will best address our concerns. In our reporting of the issues involved in the 1996 race, we have learned to be cautious about claiming that one issue or the other is the driving force behind the changes that face us. In 1856 the looming war between the states of the Union and questions about what would happen after that war was resolved could not have been foreseen by voters then, preoccupied as they were by more emotional questions about slavery, land settlement policy, and the boundaries of new states.

Today we call such emotional points of disagreement *hot-button issues* because they tend to fire our emotions and cloud our ability to see past them to what is really at stake. This is not to disdain arguments about abortion rights, gun control, or school prayer as trivial issues. They are important. So also is the question of the size of the federal government and whether more government functions should be performed by units of government on the state or local level. But it does seem to us that the basic question that confronts the voters of 1996 is one they may not get around to deciding with any finality. Indeed, it may be an issue that remains unanswered until the presidential election of the year 2000, or perhaps beyond that.

For we have come to the conclusion that what is really at issue is not the size of government nor even the question of where government functions are to be performed. It is clear that Americans are questioning something more basic: their own role in the society in which they will live out their lives. It is the nature of American federalism that is up for redefinition. It is a question of whether the people will continue to delegate increasing power to representatives who administer in the public interest, or whether individual citizens, by themselves or in groups of special interests banded together, will more directly shape and administer the public will. For most of the history of this nation, the trend has been in one direction, and it is useful to recall just how far we have come in that direction.

There was a time in the early history of American cities
when even the most basic urban services were provided for
by individual effort and paid for out of private means
according to the wealth of the citizens. Fire brigades and
police protection, potable water and even public roads
were matters of private concern. Education was a matter
for the family; hospitals, prisons, and institutions for the
relief of the poor and homeless were the domain of religious and private charities well into this century. That
changed as the intense pressures of urban growth
demanded that government assume the delivery of these
services on a fair and equal basis to all citizens and that tax
money be raised to pay for them. We began to subsidize art
and culture and to turn to the courts to settle what once
were private differences. Well and good for the time. But
over the last twenty-five years the demand for more government services for the public good continued to expand
even as the capacity of government to satisfy that demand
began to decline. Public education began to be replaced by
private schools paid for by people who continued to pay
taxes supporting public-education facilities they feared to
use. Wealthier communities have begun to provide private
police protection and even to wall themselves in against
the threats posed by neighbors. Growing numbers of consumers now import bottled water into their homes in
preference to the water that flows from their taps and for
which they pay taxes. Perhaps most significant is that
people now live their lives so as to avoid the cities themselves; the sprawling web of exurban networks is judged a
better way in part because it insulates us from one another.

In more recent years a related trend has emerged.
Increasing numbers of communities are bypassing formal
government institutions altogether. This trend is called
"taking back the neighborhood" in some places. It is visible in neighborhood anti-crime patrols, in the reclamation

of local parks and recreation facilities, in private fund-raising drives to supplement the facilities and personnel of schools. While this trend is visible, it is episodic, and it produces uneven results because some communities have better means to solve problems than others. Operating alongside this trend is a growing demand that formal government return some of the money it has claimed in tax revenues so that citizens can use this money more productively on their own priorities; examples of this are school and housing vouchers. At its extreme, government appears to be an enemy of the people, wasting public money in inefficiencies and corruption, supporting activities that the public does not want, and failing to address problems of pressing concern. Yet the real cry is not for less government power but for more efficient solutions to serious public needs. The waste of a young life because of poor education is not an individual loss; it is a national tragedy. The spread of disease and the lack of good medical care is not a family problem; it is a threat to us all. Crime makes victims of everyone. We seek more insulated lives in part because we now live more closely together than ever. In this context, the hot-button topics have an importance larger than just the issues themselves. They are symptoms of the larger malaise that grips us.

A solution, or, more exactly, the right mix of solutions, may be a long time in coming. It takes time for issues to define themselves in the public debate. As in 1856, in 1996 one cannot identify an individual among the flock of would-be Presidents who has the ability to focus the mind of America on the essential task ahead—as, say, Franklin Roosevelt did in 1932 or John Kennedy did in 1960. Many of this season's aspirants are men whose service and attitudes are rooted in the old ways of government—which are the very notions the public appears to reject. This thin crop of candidates espouses slogans that generate emotion in some but which have the same ring of irrelevance that the slogans of bygone hot issues such as free soil, bimetalism, and Manifest Destiny have to modern ears.

Having said that, we also believe that the 1996 election is one of the most important in our history. Choices will be made, however shallow the depth of the candidate pool may be. Political power will be conferred on the chosen leaders, as in the past. And they, in turn, will attempt to lead us in directions as yet uncharted. History is not a straight-line progression toward perfection. It is not inevitable that a Lincoln or a Roosevelt will emerge at times of crisis to save us from our unreason and passions; we must save ourselves. That is what democratic elections are all about. This, then, is why we undertook to examine the individuals who seek our vote today and the issues that drive them, and us, toward tomorrow.

CAMPAIGN '96: THE ECONOMY AND SO MUCH MORE

FOR THE FIRST TIME IN LIVING MEMORY, BOTH THE Republicans and the Democrats are praying that the economy will be in fine fettle when the 1996 presidential election occurs on November 5.

President Bill Clinton *must* have a healthy economy if he is to convince voters to forget his shaky first term and give him another. Republicans need prosperity, too, if they are to convince the middle ground of voters to take a chance on the GOP's radical course change for America's future.

What scares political strategists of both camps is the nightmare that if the economy is too deeply in recession (or if some external crisis frightens the voters), one of a number of third-party alternatives could capture the public imagination. Ross Perot proved in 1992 that the American electorate is split into three virtually equal camps and that the margin of victory is in the hands of a disaffected, volatile, very cranky group of working-class independents. Pollsters are just now acknowledging that the 1994 swing to the right was not solely caused by angry white men. Rather, they recognize that a demographic group they call "Some College" was the section of the population that changed its mind most dramatically between 1992 and 1994. This group is what its name implies—Americans who were unable to complete their college education and who hold a fragile grip in the workplace somewhere between lower-level white-collar salaries and blue-collar wages. Women dominate this group, not men. They voted for Bill Clinton in 1992 because he promised to expand job opportunities and to improve the safety-net programs for children and health care. Accusations about Clinton's sex and business adventures have clouded his image with women, and his failure to improve their personal economic prospects moved them to the right two years later. For Clinton to capture these swing voters, there had better be prosperity, or there will be trouble.

Americans also will have a chance to vote on whether they really want a new system of government. The choice is not between big government or no government. Not even the most radical on the right want to do more than pare some of Washington's bureaucratic excesses. Those who argue that states and cities should be given back some of the federal government's power still expect local government to exercise that power in an active way that would have been unthinkable earlier in this century. What is wanted is more efficient government, not anarchy. Not even GOP demands for abolishing the Department of Energy, to cite just one example, call for ending the $11 billion in federal grants to the states or any of the other programs that make up 90 percent of the agency's $35 billion budget.

So what, then, do Americans *really* want? Is it a paradoxical yen for a reduction in the size of the federal government just as long as social safety nets for the poor, the sick, and the elderly are preserved? Are Americans ready to be more active and responsible in the public business of educating their children, preserving their communities' infrastructure, and building prosperity after several generations of looking to Washington to make the choices?

Listen to Frank Luntz, one of the leading polltakers for the Republicans. "In 1986, 55 percent of Americans felt it would be more difficult for the next generation to attain the American dream. Today, 78 percent hold that view, and only 14 percent expect attaining the dream to get easier. This outlook is equally bleak across all age, income, education, and racial subgroups," he told us.

Now listen to President Bill Clinton: "Middle-class values, strong families and faith, safe streets, secure futures–these things are very much threatened today . . . threatened by thirty years of social problems of profound implications . . . threatened by the failure of public institutions to respond, the failure of bureaucracies encrusted in yesterday's prerogatives and not meeting the challenges of today and tomorrow." It is a comment that could have been drafted by the master theorist of the new Republican insurgency, House Speaker Newt Gingrich. The idea is ratified by widespread public-opinion polls showing that 85 percent of Americans believe their elected officials in Washington are out of touch with their constituency; indeed, the advantages that once came with political incumbency are now seen as a liability. Nearly two-thirds of American voters believe that newly elected officials are better than experienced politicians at carrying out the public will. Only one American in three now believes that "most elected officials care what people like me think," down nearly half from seven years ago.

It is a grim consensus. *Something* has gone wrong. Whatever the successes of the era of New Deal–Great Society government, changes must be made. And there is surprising agreement throughout the political spectrum that something revolutionary is under way.

The phrase *postmodern society* is commonly used by

both sides to describe the new vision of a truly global village of real-time information trading and volatile financial flows across huge distances around the world. This is what Alvin and Heidi Toffler, the authors of *Future Shock,* have called "the politics of the Third Wave" in describing the new environment we all are moving into as the Industrial Revolution, which shaped the nineteenth and twentieth centuries, yields to the Information Age, which will shape the twenty-first.

"Third Wave nations sell information and innovation, management, cultural and pop culture, advanced technology, software, education, training, medical care and financial and other services to the world. One of those services might well also turn out to be military protection based on their command of superior Third Wave forces. That is, in effect, what the high-tech nations provided for Kuwait and Saudi Arabia in the Gulf War," the Tofflers explain. Interestingly, the foreword to their book is written by another deep thinker about the future, Newt Gingrich.

Like all futurists, the Tofflers are way ahead of the curve. The upcoming vote will bypass for the time being a host of complicated foreign-policy and strategic-defense questions. The focus of Election '96 is on America as people want it to be.

One of the immediate problems is that not everyone's voice is contributing to the debate. Voters can only choose between candidates who are actually in the race. Many potential Republican candidates and a far larger number of Democrats are sitting out the early stages, hoping all of the front-runners will fall, while others have flung their hats into the ring this time around mostly in order to round up supporters in preparation for the 2000 election.

This brings us to the first bit of bad news about the 1996 election: It may not settle anything.

Both major parties are about to offer candidates who are

more targets of the coming changes than leaders of that change. Remember that it was President Clinton, as the governor of Arkansas, who helped found the Democratic Leadership Council (DLC), which seeks to move away from old-style party coalition politics and to chart a new middle way. Yet today the DLC denounces Clinton for having abandoned their cause for the far left wing of the party. Bob Dole is a self-proclaimed Eisenhower Republican, and even his leading challengers, such as Phil Gramm and Lamar Alexander, are scarcely advocates of the radical solutions offered by Newt Gingrich and his cadre of seventy-three militant Congressional freshmen.

Not surprisingly, tempers are already short and resentments are large throughout both the Democratic and Republican parties. Both parties face a number of rebellions within their own ranks and then the daunting prospect of more than one independent challenge. The prospect of a number of narrow-focus, Perot-style insurgencies in the general election raises the disturbing prospect that no presidential candidate may claim a majority or even as narrow an electoral mandate as Clinton did four years ago. While the voters want a clear decision, they may have to settle for some sort of brokered coalition. For the first time in this century, there is an outside chance that the election could be thrown into the House of Representatives and that the resulting horse trading could deteriorate into an unforeseen and unwelcome period of European-style coalition governments in America.

It seems that none of the formerly large blocs of voters seen in past elections can stick together anymore. Nowhere is the division of opinion more stark than among African-Americans, where factions are backing active presidential bids by the Reverend Jesse Jackson, on the left; by Arthur Fletcher, the Nixon-era civil-rights commissioner who began affirmative-action enforcement, on the right; and by radio commentator Alan Keyes, even farther right.

Most opinion-polling experts for both parties agree that neither the Democrats nor the Republicans can be entirely sure of the total loyalty of their usual supporters. On the left, the traditional clients of Democratic social agendas often fail to turn out at the polls. Voters oriented toward particular social-conscience issues may also stray unless the Democratic candidates score 100 percent on these voters' checklists. Libertarians and the militant churchgoers, usually found in the GOP ranks, are notorious sulkers, too. The most volatile group is in the center, among independents and those distrustful of the political system—the voters who once congregated around Ross Perot.

So positive consensus will not be easy. Perhaps that is why politics is more akin to geological phenomena than military campaigns. After all, the 1994 earthquake that rocked Capitol Hill began as a small series of tectonic tremors as far back as 1976, when that early outsider President, Jimmy Carter, first campaigned to bring government under control. This was the time of grassroots revolts, of Proposition 13 and other bids to make lawmakers bend to the public will. It was also during this time that Everett Ladd, the director of the Roper Center for Public Opinion Research, wrote, "The New Deal has become history."

The tremors grew in frequency and power during the Reagan-Bush era. The shattering November 1994 congressional upheaval must be seen as just one significant episode in an ongoing challenge to the basic assumptions about what governments–all governments–are supposed to do for their citizenry. In that sense, the 1996 election is part of an experiment that will continue on into the next century.

The challenge before the voters is directly aimed at central governments and at the elaborate ties between bureaucracies and old-style political groupings of citizens. Opinion polls sponsored by both political parties have turned up a dramatic insistence that people want to be treated more as individuals, to have more personal freedom, to make more choices about their personal lives within the framework of a society in which government is more efficient, less intrusive, and less wedded to political dogma.

Part of this phenomenon is deeply rooted in the American character. As pollster Ladd notes, recent surveys "show the U.S. public [is] consistently less inclined than citizens of most other industrial nations to turn to government for various guarantees and assistance." Yet the challenge is going on outside America, too. Throughout the industrial world, entrenched political party establishments are finding that the old blandishments of social welfare and economic tinkering no longer work. In nearby Canada the Conservative Party, dominant since World War II, nearly vanished a year ago in parliamentary elections that swung not to the left but rather to a hastily fabricated centrist coalition. France, Italy, and Japan all have dumped their longtime ruling parties into the minority. In Britain, the Labour Party has had to forswear its socialist manifesto just to be a credible opposition to the Tories, who themselves are divided.

Americans too no longer want what they once craved. The makeup of the country has changed, and one of the ironies of that change is that the very political groupings that both sustained and were beneficiaries of the social-welfare efforts of the past sixty years are now among the most ungrateful.

Consider how the Democratic party has changed.

- Labor unions now account for roughly 15 percent of non-farm workers, half the share they had in 1948.

- The urban coalitions of ethnic minorities that dominated the big cities of the Northeast and Midwest have seen their impact halved as well, as families moved to the suburbs and even to other regions in the country. Once moved, these voters changed their political attitudes as dramatically as their addresses.
- The American South, which received an enormous share of New Deal largesse fifty years ago, is now solidly Republican; so too are the states of the Far West, where the federal government has provided vast land subsidies and most of the water that fueled the development boom there.

Not that the Republicans are the same as they once were.

- The old coalition of country-club and Farm Belt Republicans has shrunk to an even greater degree than has the coalition of unions and Democrats. Pollsters refer to this vanishing group of GOP loyalists as "enterprisers," but these affluent, pro-business, anti-government voters now account for less than 12 percent of the voting population. One of the big defections from the traditional GOP base is among the chief executives of America's biggest corporations, who long ago learned how to thrive during Democratic presidencies—including how to profit from government subsidies and how their firms could avoid Democratic restraints.
- The libertarians, who formerly held the intellectual high ground with their least-government-is-best theories, have undergone a philosophical change as they become more pro-business and more willing to debate on social issues.

- Most dramatic has been the transformation of the
  moral right, which used to be typified by evange-
  list Billy Graham and the established churches.
  These older moralists limited themselves to pro-
  moting a generic standard of religious morality
  on such issues as peace and civil rights. Today's
  Christian right is not content just to remind
  politicians to be more moral. The Christian
  Coalition, directed by Ralph Reed, wants to have
  a say in all the major issues, from abortion rights
  and school prayer to tax policy and health care.
  These moralists tend also to be against both big
  government *and* big business.

So one transformation to keep watch for is the evolution
of the two major parties themselves. Democrat and
Republican politicians alike have become part of a system
of government that many Americans appear not to want
anymore. The divisions within both parties threaten to push
the old-style pols out to the margins of the real battle.
When Bill Clinton argues for more government power to
cure what ails big government, he is missing the point.
When Republicans debate bills to abolish unwanted federal
bureaucracies by transferring their functions to other boxes
on the government organization chart, they are missing the
point, too, and not fooling the voters at all.

The 1996 Presidential election season will be hard to
endure. Nearly thirty years of bipartisan efforts to open up
our electoral system to involve more citizens, to curb the
power of special interests, and to rid campaign funding of
its corrupt unfairness have accomplished little of what they
set out to do; rather, they have had some significant unintended consequences.

Consider this: America now has a primary system that caters more to television than to open choice. The crucial part of the selection process for the two major parties will be compressed into just forty-six days (February 12 through March 26), when all the major state delegations will be chosen. By early May, 70 percent of the delegates to the Republican convention in San Diego (August 10–16) and the Democrats' Chicago conclave (August 26–29) will already be committed. The rush to be first with the most delegates has diluted the debate on issues to a glib exchange of sound bites.

As for the reform of campaign-finance rules, intended to attract a greater number of smaller contributors, the effect has been just the opposite. Most candidates now are hostages to newly powerful consultants who prepare mass mailings soliciting contributions. Oliver North is one example; largely through out-of-state mail solicitations, he raised more than $20 million for his 1994 Virginia Senate race. At the same time, Ross Perot and Michael Huffington are just two of an increasing number of wealthy candidates who have opted out of any control on spending altogether by investing millions of their own wealth in order to avoid the federal limits.

The end product of campaign-finance reform is a dismal slate of possible presidential choices that hardly makes voters enthusiastic about the outcome. The main advantage that most of the front-runners of both parties have is that they started early enough in 1995 to raise the $25 million or more that each must have just to ante up for the early round of primaries in the spring of 1996. Even though the federal presidential campaign spending limit for candidates who accept government matching funds is $47 million, the next presidency may cost the winner $100 million once "soft dollars" (unlimited support to party and political action groups) are counted. Each of the losers will have to spend almost as much.

And for what? one might ask.

Bill Clinton is a sincerely well-intentioned President. Yet, depending on the prevailing wind, he swings from grandiose liberal nostrums to a "lite" version of the GOP Contract with America. While he probably is the best political campaigner of this season, he has pleased almost no one on the issues that define his presidency. Worse, he has been hampered by a Cabinet that, except for one or two members, has been overwhelmed by the bureaucracies they were supposed to bring to heel. His White House team regularly confuses opinion polling results with substantive political leadership. While Jesse Jackson or some other party radical may challenge the President, most of the new-style Democrats who hold the party's center prefer to sit out the 1996 campaign, waiting for the *real* test of strength that will occur in the year 2000.

Yet it is plausible that Bill Clinton could win a second term, if only because the American voters would rather endure a disappointing President they know than take a risk on a Republican nominee who frightens rather than inspires them.

For their part, the Republican front-runners appear to be ignoring the mandate that swept their party into full control of both houses of the U.S. Congress for the first time since 1946. Bob Dole represents an Eisenhower-style cautious moderation that was discarded by Republicans after Gerald Ford's loss in 1976. Further to the right, rivals such as Phil Gramm and Pat Buchanan play a more-conservative-than-thou game. Still others in the pack prefer simply to stand around, hoping that the front-runners will stumble and fall on the campaign trail.

If there is a motto for the 1996 election, "less is more" seems appropriate. Both President Clinton and his rivals agree that a smaller, less intrusive, more responsive federal government is what is needed. The argument then rests on which method should be used to do the trimming—the sharper, deeper cuts proposed by the freshman Republicans elected in the 1994 sweep of the House, the governors' mansions, and the state legislatures; the not-so-deep cuts of the Senate Republicans; or President Clinton's less draconian version. The question is not so much over the optimal size of the Washington establishment but over who should wield its power. Clinton and most Democrats want to keep the power where it is—in Washington. Republicans want to shift many of government's responsibilities to state and local governments and to put more choices into the hands of voters.

However, while most political pundits are looking for dramatic change to come out of Washington, there are early signals that much of the new thinking about how we will order our lives in the future is now going on in state capitals and in city halls across the land. This may indicate that some parts of the radical Republican agenda are producing changes, albeit outside the Beltway. For example, welfare rolls in states where governors are already committed to new workfare experiments and time limits on support have seen a remarkable drop in claims for benefits. Wisconsin governor Tommy Thompson's plan to tie aid to single mothers to their going back to school is being used as a model in other states. In the three months before new, tougher eligibility rules were put into effect by Virginia governor George Allen, the welfare rolls shrank by 5,800 claimants who presumably saw the ax coming and adjusted accordingly.

In that respect, the radical revolution of American politics has already achieved one of its most important objectives. Time was when most of the creative ideas about how America should operate came out of Washington and were the province of one party, the Democrats. That is certainly history now. Another development is the decline in importance of political labels. To be sure, the Republicans have not sewn up their claim to be the sole authors of political change, but the Democrats will have to fight hard to reclaim their traditional role in this respect.

But these may be small matters. What is important is that for the first time in a long while, politicians are scrambling to find out what America wants. That is what the political revolution is really all about, anyway. The process may be a noisy one, but the results may not be all that bad.

Part One

CANDIDATES

PRESIDENT AGAIN—IF . . .

NAME: William Jefferson Clinton
BORN: August 19, 1946
EDUCATION: B.A., Georgetown University; J.D., Yale University
OCCUPATION: President of the United States
FAMILY: Married to Hillary Rodham Clinton; one child
QUOTE: "There is a difference between reputation and character. I have increasingly less control over my reputation but still full control over my character."

PRESIDENT BILL CLINTON HAS ENTERED HIS 1996 reelection campaign as a modified version of his 1992 campaign self: a moderate-to-liberal Democrat. How he returned to his political roots has been an interesting process to witness, particularly given one charge against him—that there's no *there* there, no core beliefs.

As President, Clinton has been an affable bull in a political china shop, bumping into things, changing his mind, spinning around as something new attracts or demands his attention, asking, "What's that? What's that?" He loves to acquire knowledge for its own sake, and in some ways his presidency to date can be seen as one long seminar—punctuated with bursts of anticipated and unanticipated action. Close up,

Clinton is like everyone's favorite college professor: simultaneously curious and pragmatic, interested in what's being said and in opposing views, and extremely candid about his own opinions and failings.

But early in 1995, with a campaign on the calendar for later in the year, Clinton began to decide on which political turf he would stand and on which issues he was going to drive his stake into the ground and refuse to budge. In February, in one of those low-key sessions he's noted for—eight journalists plus himself in the Oval Office–he made himself clear on a tough topic: welfare reform. He told us he would not let welfare reform punish innocent children (meaning he'd oppose Republican plans to ban additional payments for additional children born to a mother already on welfare). That same month, other meetings laid the groundwork that would result in Clinton's defense in late July of affirmative action.

Welfare and affirmative action—not the most popular of causes. What was happening?

That became clear early in July, when Clinton returned to his alma mater, Georgetown University. There he reaffirmed who and what he was: a baby boomer proud of his generation and its activism on behalf of racial equality, the poor, and the undereducated. This was a theme he had made clear in February as well, when he said, "In the sixties, important advances in civil rights, education, and fighting poverty really made a difference. In the seventies we made a national commitment as a country to defend our environment. This is a safer, cleaner, healthier place because of what we've done for the last twenty-five years."

During his Georgetown talk the President contrasted his own approach to solving the nation's problems to that of the Republicans, and he did not shy away from saying that there was indeed a role for an activist federal government. That was deliberate, for this Georgetown address was the pivotal point in his 1996 reelection bid. Quietly, humorously, and self-deprecatingly, as is often his wont, he defended his version of the middle-class American dream. He expounded on his vision for economic, social, and political progress and applauded the more noble actions and attributes of his generation.

It was appropriate that Georgetown University was where this reaffirmation took place. It was from Georgetown that student Clinton had gone to help Washington, D.C., clean up after the riots of the 1960s, and it was from the same university that Rhodes scholar Clinton had gone to England, where he protested against the Vietnam War and helped organize an interfaith prayer service for all who were being injured by it.

Government has to be involved, Clinton told the Georgetown audience. He is convinced that in order "to create more opportunity and demand more responsibility, to have middle-class dreams and middle-class values, we have to do things in partnership—through public agencies and through other associations.

"In 1994, when the Republicans won a majority in Congress," he continued, "they offered a different view. . . . Their contract [the Contract with America] viewed most of our problems [as] personal and cultural; the government tended to make [problems] worse because it was bureaucratic and wedded to the past, and more interested in regulating and choking off the free-enterprise system," Clinton said. As Clinton interprets it, Gingrich's new Congress seeks to "balance the budget as soon as possible, deregulate business completely if possible, and cut things like our investment in welfare as much as possible."

By contrast, the President said, he believes there are "things we could do here in Washington to help, whether family leave, or tougher child-support enforcement, or pension system reform, or investing more in education, or making college more affordable. My whole political philosophy is basically rooted in what I think works."

And it was from Georgetown, after this speech, that President Clinton went back to the White House and stood up for what he thinks works. He dug in his heels over the GOP's "unacceptable cuts" in his social programs—cuts that through his chief of staff, Leon Panetta, he threatened to veto—and signed legislation restoring relations with Vietnam.

As these examples show, Clinton can hang tough—though frequently he hasn't. He's stuck to his guns before: As governor of Arkansas, for instance, he pushed through a highly unpopular testing program for teachers in his determination to upgrade the state's abysmal educational ratings. And as President, he has not backed down on AmeriCorps (his national service corps) and does not hesitate to defend federal activism in job-skills training or education initiatives.

William Jefferson Clinton, forty-second President of the United States, was born in Hope, Arkansas, on August 19, 1946, the *Dobie Gillis* generation's first President. Clinton's initial successful election bid was as Georgetown freshman-class president; his early defeats came when he ran for high-school senior-class secretary and in a 1973 congressional bid.

Having won election in 1976 as Arkansas attorney general, two years later Clinton, at thirty-two, became the state's youngest governor. He was defeated in 1980, and reelected again in 1982 for another two years. Arkansas increased the governor's term to four years and Clinton's subsequent reelection kept him in office until 1988. He decided against a presidential run in 1988 and instead gave the Democratic convention nominating speech for Michael Dukakis.

During the 1992 campaign the character issue of his alleged extramarital affair surfaced. He and his wife, Hillary Rodham Clinton, appealed on *60 Minutes* for their "zone of privacy" to be respected. To some extent, the tactic worked.

Later, baby boomer Clinton won 43 percent of the general-election vote against 38 percent for incumbent President George Bush and 19 percent for billionaire Ross Perot—each of whom was old enough to be his father.

What sort of politician is the First Boomer? Pragmatic. His supporters may talk of a certain consistency to his style, honed over three decades, but it's essentially one dedicated to getting elected.

The affable and gregarious Clinton really does like people. All politicians rely on friends, but Clinton's friends and top campaigners are part of a non-stop free-floating seminar that involves them completely. The White House is a talk-talk-talk milieu that drove General Colin Powell—highly attuned to order and procedure in discussions—to distraction when he was Chairman of the Joint Chiefs of Staff.

The clear-eyed political Clinton will turn to anyone he needs for help. Always has. Richard Morris, the political consultant with far more right-of-center Republicans on his Rolodex and resumé than Democrats, first appeared in Clinton's life after Arkansas Governor Clinton was rejected for reelection in 1980.

By mid-1995, Morris, the man who taught Clinton how to apologize to the electorate, was back. He's masterminding the Clinton campaign. Clinton hasn't apologized for telling Americans they were in a funk. What he was telling Americans, but he said it poorly, was about their own inconsistencies. He'd aired the topic of the electorate's split personality before. Examples abound, as Clinton sees them.

"I believe the majority of Americans are pro-choice and

anti-abortion," he has said several times. "They don't
believe the decision should be penalized—because there
are too many different circumstances. On the other hand,
most people feel, in most circumstances, that abortion is
wrong."

During one session with a handful of journalists, the
President took the electorate's inner conflict further, this
time on elections. "The American people respond to negative things (like character assassination), but they don't like
it," he argued, obviously enjoying himself. "The reason it
keeps happening is *because* they respond—politicians
know the negatives work to elect people. So the people
respond, but they hate it."

One largely overlooked dimension of the President's
character, because the general media are secular institutions, is the religion facet. Journalists frequently are aston-
ished at the ease and the humor with which he brings God
and belief and religion into the conversation.

Talking to a few reporters, he mentioned he'd been reading the Book of Psalms and wryly remarked on how David
was "praying for the strength to be purified in the face of
adversity and in the face of his own failings." This came at
a moment when his own past sexual conduct was receiving
another airing, in David Maranis's book, *The First in His
Class: A Biography of Bill Clinton.*

Yet he leaned forward in his Oval Office armchair, and
continued on. "I need the power of God. This is—a humble
thing for me. It's an important part of my life, especially in
recent years. The same thing is true for Hillary."

Three religious traditions shape Clinton: his own
Southern Baptist upbringing, Roman Catholicism (grade
school under the nuns; Georgetown under the Jesuits), and
Hillary Rodham's Methodism. Yet, he explained, "there
are people who don't believe it's genuine because they disagree with me politically. They don't believe you can be a

committed Christian and not want to criminalize all abortions. They don't believe you can be a committed Christian and take the position I took on gays in the military."

Religion has never been far from Clinton's politics. In Arkansas campaigns, he leaned heavily on the support of African-American clergy. It was only after he entered the White House, and became the Religious Right's preferred enemy for his stances on abortion and gays in the military, that he began the broader public discourse, inviting religious groups in to talk.

In small groups, Clinton has a near-genius for making people feel not just at ease but equal.

Enemies, by contrast, see this as the cynical glad-handing of a smooth schmoozer. Other critics see Clinton as the ultimate pragmatist—the only end is to be elected.

There are those, his closest backers, though, who see consistency in this man from his Rhodes Scholar days at Oxford when he anguished over Vietnam; Clinton the compassionate listener; Clinton, always incredibly well informed.

His widely touted ability to rapidly absorb facts also is genuine—he can pore over reports, and very quickly convert his mental notes into a cohesive position.

But too often—and it is a habit that has followed him down the decades—he throws that position back into the debate, and the seminar starts up all over again. He loves political and intellectual wrangling in the White House today just as much as the Georgetown and Oxford into-the-night bull sessions.

And because they were in the original intellectual free-for-alls and liked what they saw and heard, after three decades many of those same collegians are still with him, such as Labor Secretary Robert Reich and Deputy Secretary of State Strobe Talbott.

Also debating him, or disagreeing with him, or driving

him on politically—ever since his first successful public campaign as Arkansas attorney general in 1976—is his wife, Hillary Rodham Clinton.

And here the conventional wisdom is undoubtedly correct, that she is totally involved in all aspects of his political career—pragmatic enough to know what can and cannot be done, though not as pragmatic as her husband. She does pull him to the left—for she is the quintessential Methodist. She is, as one Washingtonian described her, "a terrific person, absolutely driven, smart as can be and a believer in John Wesley's public gospel." By that he meant Methodism as the spiritual rebuttal to the worst of the Industrial Revolution.

Hillary Rodham is as take-charge as her husband—her health care reform role was only one indication of that. Another, as Maranis states in his book, is that Mrs. Clinton has had to worry about maintaining or augmenting the family income. Her husband's financial interests seem to falter once he gets beyond the fundraising necessary for the next election. If she pragmatically yields when Clinton, as now, is being drawn to the middle or right-of-center, she accepts that as political necessity. How their own debates shape up in the family quarters of the White House is one of the great unknowns.

Once in the White House, as National Economic Council deputy director Gene Sperling tells it, Clinton pushed to achieve five main objectives. The President "came in and he said that he was going to bring down the deficit, which he did," says Sperling. "When we came in, the Congressional Budget Office estimated that the [annual] deficit was going to be $653 billion in the year 2003—on a path that headed nowhere but up. The President laid out his plan twenty-seven days after he took office. It was the first successful deficit plan. People can argue about whether it's going down fast enough or getting toward zero fast enough, but in seven years it's going to reduce the deficit a trillion off of what was projected before we came here."

Former Congressional Budget Office director Robert Reischauer, now a Brookings Institute scholar, agrees. In giving the Clinton administration "pretty high marks" on the domestic economy, Reischauer calls Clinton's deficit reduction "a courageous and successful move" for which the administration was "punished," yet "the actions that it took did and will lead to lower deficits."

Two other Clinton successes, Reischauer says, were stimulating the economy, "which was experiencing a rather lackluster rebound from the '91 recession," and "reorienting spending priorities so that more emphasis was placed on government investment and on spending on behalf of certain vulnerable populations." Even so, Reischauer still regards deficit reduction as the top economic issue before the nation.

Clinton also stressed that he was going to make major new investments in education and training programs. The President "stayed true to his putting-people-first agenda," Sperling notes. "The Goals 2000 plan was a nationwide effort to have local governments come up with plans for accountability and standards for teachers." The school-to-work program is a high school-based work-release program to equip students for the blue collar, technician and service jobs market. Clinton also proposed a new direct lending program for educational loans, which gave students the opportunity to borrow at lower cost and also to pay the loans back in monthly amounts contingent upon their future income.

"Number three, we were going to open markets and have a more open trade system, which we have," continues Sperling. "When we came in, NAFTA [the North American Free Trade Agreement] and GATT [the General

Agreement on Tariffs and Trade] were in very bad situations. Nobody would have bet on them at that point." And for those energetic trade policies Clinton has gained many kudos, corporate and otherwise.

The fourth goal, Sperling says, was that "we were going to promote rewarding work, which we have through the earned-income tax credit." The Clinton administration succeeded in winning a $21 billion increase in the earned-income tax credit for 15 million families near the poverty line.

The fifth item on Clinton's agenda was health-care reform. Sperling says that the failure of the President's plan was "a major disappointment—but we did a lot to create a national debate, a national dialogue on the issue."

If President Clinton is reelected, expect more of the same, economically speaking. There'll be another try for health-care reform; a similar course on deficit reduction (at the moment Clinton is saying that the deficit will be down to zero in nine years); more encouragement for high-technology industry; efforts to manage international trade; proposals for welfare reform; and more attention to education and job-skills training.

But will he get that second term? From the administration's perspective, Clinton faces two serious, almost amorphous problems: national short-term memory lapses, and a sense of personal economic foreboding experienced by many Americans.

The first problem, that of memory lapses, says Sperling, means that the administration's economic successes go unrecognized or are too easily forgotten.

The other problem was one Clinton himself addressed at Georgetown. "It all seems so confusing," he said. The United States has been experiencing "the highest growth rates in a decade, the stock market at an all-time high, almost seven million new jobs, more millionaires and new businesses than ever before." Yet, he went on, "most people [are] working harder for less, feeling more insecure."

Here he is three months later in the Cabinet Room amplifying the same theme at a Sept. 15, 1995, roundtable discussion. "Since I've been President and we put in our economic policy," he said, "we've had 7.3 million new jobs, 2.5 million new home owners, two million new businesses—record numbers—a record number of self-made millionaires, the stock market at 4,700, record corporate profits, the unemployment of African Americans below 10 percent for the first time in 20 years—since the end of the Vietnam War—and [yet] the median wage dropped one percent—almost inconceivable. In the midst of all this economic growth, another million Americans each year lost their health insurance."

And it is that anxiety about the economy that will determine Clinton's political future. Whitewater, a potential trade war with Japan, conflicts with China, a possible Bosnia debacle, battles over a balanced budget—probably none of these is enough to cause Clinton to lose the White House. After all, this is the man whom even Bob Dole calls "the comeback kid" (the title of Charles Allen's biography of the President). Even Newt Gingrich told television interviewer Charlie Rose that you can't count Clinton out—"he can be reelected."

Big business likes him. Big corporate money is flowing into Clinton's 1996 reelection bid coffers. Reasons abound. He stood up to Japan on luxury cars, his Commerce Department has pushed hard for big U.S. multinational interests.

Behind the scenes there are more complex corporate maneuverings. An oil industry insider said the Clinton Administration's recognition of Vietnam was very much tied into U.S. oil majors wanting their share of any offshore Vietnam oilfields. A Washington watcher added that

oil interests are part of the new trade liberalizations toward
Cuba, too. Clinton's October decision to allow the export
of supercomputers—despite objections that U.S. security
and technology might be jeopardized—played to the corporate suite.

On foreign policy—not a paramount factor in the campaigning thus far—Clinton has achieved a modest Haiti
success and may take a Bosnia risk. Committing U.S.
troops to Bosnia would require precise timing and strong
nerves—in order to get those troops out before the election
and declare a victory. But he's got the nerve—he was fifteen minutes away from sending the U.S. Marines into
Haiti. Clinton might, if Bosnia works, add a star to his
commander-in-chief's epaulette.

But the economy *can* do him in. It's not just that an economic downturn could defeat Clinton; worse yet, from the
incumbent's perspective, is the fact that the downturn
doesn't even have to be really there. It just has to feel as if
it's there. And that feeling is growing, which is precisely
the point Clinton was making at Georgetown.

He knows that hard-pressed American industrial or service
workers feel more productive than ever—and put in more
hours. Clinton understands that middle-management and
white-collar workers—at least those who are still employed
after all the downsizing—feel that their workload has probably doubled. All are grateful for their jobs, but they do not
see their extra effort or responsibility being rewarded with
increased buying power or with job security.

Here, then, is a reelection bid in which the national
mood matters as much as substance, and in which empathy
may be more important than economic priorities. One of
Clinton's main reelection strategies has to be to spin a
thicker and more durable thread of national optimism to
support the imagined economic sword of Damocles that
the individual voter senses hanging above his or her head.

To win, the President has to infect a 1990s electorate with the can-do attitude and hopefulness that was characteristic of the 1950s and 1960s.

This kind of cheerleading is one of Clinton's better roles; he has a certain felicity of phrase that comes across well on television. It may not be enough, but it's what he's got—and it may be all that he's got.

Certainly Clinton is taking a gamble with the position he's staked out. For the past several years, the polls and conventional political wisdom have been suggesting that voters oppose Clinton's stances on numerous issues. But the President is betting that the political pendulum has swung as far to the right as it's going to. And he's campaigning to jump aboard as it returns to the middle.

So the incumbent, in effect, is challenging conventional wisdom. Will the strategy succeed? It might—if there are enough people who remember and appreciate the gains the economy has made; if there are sufficient people not drawn to conservative prescriptions—which he and his fellow Democrats depict as extreme, even harsh or mean—to see him back in office; if he can convince voters to share the same optimism he professes; if . . . There are a lot of ifs.

PRIORITIES

1. Health care reform
2. Maintain course to balanced budget by 2005
3. Maintain minimum social services safety net
4. Restructure Medicare
5. Job creation; job training

EVERYONE LIKES BOB DOLE— BUT IS THAT ENOUGH?

NAME: Robert Joseph Dole
BORN: July 22, 1923
EDUCATION: B.A. and LL.B., Washburn University of Topeka
OCCUPATION: Majority leader of the U.S. Senate
FAMILY: Married to Elizabeth Hanford Dole (second marriage), who was a Reagan Cabinet official and currently heads the American Red Cross
QUOTE: "I hear people saying, there goes Bob Dole moving to the right. Well, I've already been there for some time, but they haven't noticed."

LADIES AND GENTLEMEN . . . THE VICE PRESIDENT OF the United States, the Honorable Daniel E. Lungren!

Vice president who?

In a gambit that puzzles outsiders but draws smiles from Republican insiders, Senator Robert Dole is trying to cement his lock on his party's presidential nomination by lofting a trial balloon that suggests Lungren, a pro-life conservative and popular California attorney general, might make a dandy running mate. Is this William Miller time all over again?

Well, yes and no.

Like Barry Goldwater's running mate Miller, a largely anonymous Congressman from Lockport, New York, Lungren is very conservative and largely unknown to the national media or indeed to the general voting public.

And yes, like Miller, Lungren would solve a couple of problems that vex Bob Dole as he tries to safeguard his grip on the nomination—a tough task against a field of a half-dozen rivals, two of whom (Senator Phil Gramm and broadcaster Pat Buchanan) are likely to make strong showings in the Iowa and New Hampshire primaries at the start of the campaign. If elected, Dole, now seventy-two, would be four years *older* than Ronald Reagan was at the beginning of his first term, and he is under intense pressure to declare publicly that he will serve only one term and that he will run with some named successor.

But Dole is not so stupid as to make himself a lame-duck President even before he gets nominated. Nor is he naive enough to choose a running mate who has burning presidential ambitions of his own. In that respect, Dole is mimicking Goldwater, but he's also following the lead of Richard Nixon when he elevated an unknown Maryland governor named Spiro Agnew, not to mention George Bush's pick of Dan Quayle.

But Dan Lungren is no Bill Miller. He brings plenty of pluses to the Dole campaign. His well-known conservatism would free Dole to swing a little more to the center in the presidential race. Lungren also solves the California problem; he was reelected last year with 4.2 million votes, 1.2 million more than his opponent. He likes to point out his victory margin was greater than the entire number of votes Ted Kennedy got in the entire state of Massachusetts in 1992.

This ought to make Dole an almost certain winner in the California primary event, now that Pete Wilson's early campaign effort ended with Wilson backing Dole. The

senator must have a lead in the early polls for the
California primary on March 26 if he is to be free to concentrate on the earlier but equally important Super Tuesday
contests on March 12 in Texas, Florida, and a host of other
Southern states.

Clearly Dole needs something. "It's Bob's turn" is not a
winning campaign cry. It did not work for Dole in his 1976
race as Gerald Ford's running mate or in his two previous
failures to get the presidential nomination in 1980 and 1988.
The dark fear is that while Dole certainly speaks to the heart
of the traditional Republican Party membership, he may,
like Democrat William Jennings Bryan earlier in this century, end up always the bridesmaid but never the bride.

What this boils down to is a pervasive feeling expressed
repeatedly to us by top GOP strategists that the 1996 nomination race "is Dole's to lose." Even more to the point,
Dole must win his party's banner in such a way as to rule
out any resurgence by the original comeback kid, Bill
Clinton, in November.

Richard Wirthlin, one of the most respected of
Republican strategist-consultants, summed up the state of
affairs: "If Senator Dole is as strong a year from now as he
is today, he will without question be the nominee. He
clearly has run a solid, effective strategy in the opening
months. He has made few mistakes; he has leveraged his
leadership of the Senate to speak out on issues that are of
special concern."

But history has shown that primary campaigns are not
always kind to front-runners. The convention season is a
long way away. Wirthlin agrees: "It is premature to say
Dole has the primaries locked up. Gramm would still be
considered the second-strongest candidate; although if for
some reason Dole should stumble, I think it would be a
wide-open race between Gramm and Alexander, or possibly some unannounced candidate."

Like who? "I would keep an eye on Gingrich. The other candidates, such as Pat Buchanan and Arlen Specter, have a very remote chance of securing the presidency. One of the things that will condition the race next year will be whether there is a third-party candidate. Perot is a definite contender." Part of Wirthlin's caution may stem from the fact that he was the manager of front-running Dole's ill-fated New Hampshire campaign in 1988, when George Bush scored an upset.

Cautions aside, there are worse places to be than where Dole is these days—at the front of the GOP hunt by a clear if not comfortable margin. Recent polls say 51 percent of likely Republican voters want him to be their nominee. Hardly a landslide, but remember these are opinions about primary races involving between nine and a dozen possible party rivals, each with a fractional share of loyalties.

Also, Dole likely will be a far more formidable candidate in the 1996 battles than he has been in the past. As majority leader of the Senate in opposition to a sitting President, Dole has achieved national status as a political figure–something he did not have as minority leader or even when Ronald Reagan was President. While House Speaker Newt Gingrich can claim leadership of a specific faction of the party, Dole still stands unassailed as the leader of the traditional Republican Party and as a strong claimant for the loyalties of GOP activists, state party officials, and the big-ticket financial contributors who have been noticeably stingy to other candidates thus far. In crucial New Hampshire, early polls give Dole his commanding win in both "with Newt" or "without Newt" candidate listings. Gingrich, for all his visibility, runs slightly ahead of Buchanan (9 percent to 7 percent) for a distant second place.

Who, then, is Robert Joseph Dole, and why does he think America wants him to be President?

One thing thirty-five years in the U.S. House and Senate give a man is a political record for others to study. Political scientists call Dole a "prairie conservative," a vanishing breed of Republican pledged to fiscal conservatism, progressive but limited social policies, and an internationalist view of foreign policy. From such backgrounds sprang the Republican leaders of the past fifty years, including Dwight Eisenhower and Richard Nixon.

Inbred in Dole, then, is a long history of fierce opposition to the political nostrums of the day, which to him are merely cover for a fresh round of deficit spending. It also means that Dole has a surprising record of sympathy for the plight of America's poor and disabled. Despite intense loyalty to Ronald Reagan, Dole did not hesitate to criticize the supply-side economics theory that sparked the subsequent crippling budget deficits—spending excesses that would have been even worse if Dole had not been in a position to curb some of them.

A visit to Dole's personal office in the Russell Senate Office Building shows the difference between the man and other prominent political figures. The room is decorated more as a reminder of where Dole comes from than as a sign of who he would like to be. The walls and bookcases are filled with memorabilia of his hero, Dwight Eisenhower, and other political mentors, including Richard Nixon. On one wall of his conference room is a photograph of a weathered farmer in overalls—Dole's father.

Perhaps more important, Dole has learned from the mistakes that dogged his previous attempts to gain the White House. As a younger politician he had a tendency to let loose mean-spirited quips, but he has now turned this propensity into only the occasional lapse into soft sarcasm, often directed at himself. He also used to spurn the high-flown gestures other politicians often make in order to score dramatic points with the voters; it offended his rather dry view that voters ought to pay attention to actions, not promises. Yet in 1988 he was stung bitterly in the New Hampshire primary when he refused to sign a pledge not to increase income taxes if elected, a pledge his rivals had rushed to sign. The uproar from the other candidates drowned out his efforts to argue his campaign points. This year he quickly signed just such a pledge when he first visited the Granite State as a candidate. The promise still doesn't mean anything to anyone, but Dole wasn't about to walk into that buzzsaw a second time.

Yet Dole has not been an instant convert to what might be called Gingrich radicalism. He meets regularly with the House Speaker but was noticeably quiet during the early public enthusiasm that surrounded the Contract with America. This antipathy goes back a long way, to 1985, when he was in the lead to push the complex legislation for one of the toughest deficit-reduction packages through the Senate. The bill deferred Social Security increases for a year, eliminated thirteen domestic spending programs, and would have cut the deficit by $300 billion over three years. The bill came unstuck when Gingrich and Jack Kemp balked on the bill in the House because it did not contain massive tax cuts, which would have erased most of the budget gains. He still considers that Gingrich and Kemp betrayed him in that fight—but, significantly, he intends to make good use of them if he is elected President.

He also has ill-concealed scorn for his closest rival for the nomination, Senator Phil Gramm, who for his part charges that Dole temporizes on the hot-button issues that define radical conservatism.

"Every time Phil Gramm breathes, people say I am moving to the right. Phil can say whatever he pleases, but then, he is not a leader. It is easy to say what he says when you don't take on the responsibilities of leadership," Dole says acidly.

What would a Dole presidency look like?

It would involve a balanced budget and an end to the multibillion-dollar annual deficits, for starters. Dole takes great pride in pushing through this summer's contentious plan to balance the budget in seven years instead of the ten urged by the Clinton White House. The net savings of this shorter deficit-reduction period: $894 billion. He also wants a balanced-budget amendment to the Constitution, a scheme that failed to pass in the Senate earlier this year. Oh, yes, and this time, tax cuts.

In an interview, Dole outlined his first-term strategy this way: "To ensure that the budget stays balanced, we must also do more than just reduce spending. We must fundamentally restructure the federal government by eliminating obsolete programs, agencies, and cabinet departments. I've said we should close the Departments of Housing and Urban Development, Commerce, Energy, and Education. We should ask of every program: If it didn't already exist, would we need to create it? If the answer is no, we should stop throwing good money after bad.

"Much of what these agencies do can better be done by other existing agencies or, better still, by states and local communities. Our budget resolution returns resources and power to the states and frees them to implement policies tailored to local needs. Wherever possible, we must abandon the cookie-cutter approach where Washington sets rules for the whole nation without regard to the important differences among the fifty states," Dole adds.

"We must also combine spending cuts with tax cuts. We need to cut taxes right now in order to give American families immediate relief. Our resolution calls for a $245 billion tax cut that is long overdue. It includes a $500-per-child tax credit and a cut in the capital gains tax rate to open up the flood of seed capital to entrepreneurs," he says.

The candidate demonstrates that he is not wholly deaf to the revolution of the radical Republicans–or to their leaders–by seizing on one of their important policy demands: scrapping the present income-based federal tax system.

"We ultimately will need to scrap all eight-thousand-plus pages of the tax code and rewrite our laws starting from scratch. We must put in place a tax code that is simpler, fairer, and flatter to ensure the economy continues to lead the world in innovation and job creation," Dole said in an interview.

Then he added softly, "That is why I have joined with Speaker Gingrich in asking Jack Kemp to chair a national commission on economic growth and tax reform which will review the entire tax code with an eye toward creating a pro-growth tax system that is friendly to families and entrepreneurs." Was that a twinkle of irony in his eye? Perhaps not.

But where the new GOP radicals are resolutely inward-looking on economic policy (not to mention isolationist on foreign policy), Dole remains a firm old-style internationalist. "We must harness the power of free trade to open new markets for American high-technology exports on every continent," Dole argues. To that end, he fought with Senator Gramm and others who sought to block both NAFTA and the reorganization of the World Trade Organization. Says Dole, "The United States must lead the way toward the ultimate goal of free trade across all borders."

This is vintage Bob Dole, and such a philosophy has served him well in the past.

Dole's capacity to stick to his guns yet retain flexibility came with him to Washington in 1961 as a newly elected congressman from the Sixth District of Kansas. He was the prototype Republican of the day, opposing most of what he saw as the spendthrift experiments of the Kennedy-Johnson era–most but not all. He voted predictably for more largesse for the American farmer, but he also voted to extend food aid to the hungry and for rehabilitation programs for the handicapped. He broke GOP ranks in 1964 with votes for the Civil Rights Act and again in 1965 for the Voting Rights Act. He campaigned successfully for a vacant Kansas Senate seat in 1968 and was rewarded by Richard Nixon for his staunch support of the President's Vietnam policies by being made the highly visible chairman of the Republican National Committee for the 1972 reelection campaign. During that bitter campaign, and in the even more hotly contested race in 1976, when he ran as Gerald Ford's vice president, Dole acquired his hatchet-man reputation for his often cruel–and often disastrous–quips and harsh accusations against his opponents. He most bitterly regrets a debate with Jimmy Carter's teammate, Walter Mondale, in which he referred to "all the Democratic wars of this century."

That was twenty years ago, and Bob Dole today has emerged as a smoother, more statesmanlike political leader who now wins praise from both sides of the Senate aisle for being an honest broker on tense partisan issues with the understandably testy Democratic opposition. He still clings to his advocacy for the disadvantaged and regularly faces down colleagues such as Senator Jesse Helms on proposed cuts for food stamps and school lunches.

Dole comes by that sympathy honestly. He remembers the poverty he suffered during his youth, poverty that forced his parents to move the family into the basement of their home in Russell, Kansas, so they could rent out the upper rooms to oil-field workers.

In one of the rare displays of emotion he allows himself these days, Dole recalls, "When I was a county attorney, I had to approve the welfare list each month, and my grandparents were on that list, not through any fault of their own. They believed idleness was a sin. They were tenant farmers, kicked off the land in the Depression, and they never made it back."

Dole pushed his own way out of that cycle of despair, but not without considerable pain and suffering along the way. During World War II, Dole earned a slew of decorations for heroism, and he also suffered near-fatal injuries while serving with the 10th Mountain Division in Italy. He spent the next three years in a series of hospitals and never did recover more than partial use of his paralyzed right arm. Much of the pain and anguish of that ordeal was kept bottled up inside him, and he used it to fuel a drive for success that saw him work on a law degree even as he was serving as a Kansas state legislator and county attorney.

If Dole is considerably mellower these days, much of the credit rests with Elizabeth Hanford Dole, his second wife, whom he married in 1975. Among other calming influences, Elizabeth Dole helped her husband come to terms with his physical handicaps to the point where he now confronts them openly when he speaks to other disabled persons.

Liddy Dole is a peppy powerhouse North Carolinian who has such a formidable record of her own in Washington that some political observers have suggested that if the position of First Lady were ever made subject to popular vote, she might get into the White House ahead of her husband. In that career she has served in some major capacity in every administration going back to Lyndon Johnson. Richard Nixon made her a Federal Trade Commission member, and Ronald Reagan made her secretary of transportation. She currently is the chairman of the American Red Cross.

The Doles have become for the rank and file of GOP activists around the country what Gerry and Betty Ford were twenty years ago—the star couple who can be counted upon to travel thousands of miles each year to every local party fund-raiser, awards banquet, and registration campaign.

They also are the national party organization's current point of contact with the community of big-business leaders, a group that once was a GOP preserve. Not for nothing do the Doles have a Florida retreat in the same exclusive condominium development as party advisor and former Tennessee senator Howard Baker, and Dwayne Andreas, CEO of Archer-Daniels-Midland. The three families regularly organize holiday gatherings to which other high-powered guests are invited.

So Bob Dole is not just a member of the GOP establishment. Now that George Bush is gone from the scene, Dole is *the* leader not only of that exclusive club known as the U.S. Senate but of the top hierarchy of the party itself. He likes it that way, and he thinks he's good at his job. Anyone who wants to take it away from him will have to do more than come up with a nice-sounding platform.

But it is that very king-of-the-hill position that makes Dole vulnerable. The trick is to keep getting stronger and to keep moving; if he stands still, the ground might erode from underneath him. Dole is the man all the other Republican challengers are aiming at. They charge they are more faithfully conservative than he, that they would not make the kind of pragmatic compromises that Dole routinely agrees to in the course of moving real legislation through a real-time Senate.

A vexing case in point is the congressional struggle to rein in the powers of the large number of federal regulatory agencies. No one likes the bill that has been proposed. Liberals see it as an attempt to turn evil market riggers, environmental despoilers, and food and drug adulterers loose on the public without adequate government policing. Conservatives hate the bill because it does not go far enough and abolish many onerous rules altogether.

What Dole did was enter into a partnership with Senator Bennett Johnston, a Louisiana Democrat with strong ties to the oil and chemical industries. What the Dole-Johnston compromise bill would do is force many regulatory agencies to conduct a rigid cost-benefit calculation and other extensive analyses before setting a new rule into place. Even the bill's supporters acknowledge that the bill could add up to four years to the process of adding new regulation.

When even such a rock-ribbed conservative think tank as the Heritage Foundation calls the Dole bill "a regulatory reform setback," one can see the level of heat the plan has generated. The Heritage Foundation and other analysts on the right attack the plan for failing to do much to reduce current bureaucratic burdens and for giving regulators too much leeway in determining the least costly alternative to a rule and the reason for it at all.

Dole's clear affinity for his friends in Fortune 500 corporations will also lay him open to bitter criticism by the Democrats should he win the nomination in the summer. A Dole nomination would allow President Clinton's strategists to position their candidate as the man fighting for the little people. The hoary old clichés about country-club Republicans living off the blood and sweat of working people would not only grate on Dole but would also distract voters from what is really going on in the 1996 election.

Dole relishes a fight, of course, so he is undaunted about going toe to toe with Bill Clinton. Indeed, he would rather be about that task right now. But for the time being he must concentrate on getting the nomination locked up before June. And to do that, he needs something that will extend his lead so far that he can no longer hear the rest of the GOP pack baying at his heels.

Vice President Dan Lungren? You may have to get used to it.

<u>PRIORITIES</u>

1. Pass a balanced-budget amendment to the Constitution
2. Redistribute to the states a number of the powers and functions of the federal government
3. Reform Medicare, Medicaid, and the welfare system
4. Cut taxes for the middle class
5. Implement tough new crime-control measures
6. End U.S. subsidies of the Mexican economy
7. Strengthen NATO

THE MAVERICK WHO WOULD BE PRESIDENT

NAME: William Phillip Gramm
BORN: July 8, 1942
EDUCATION: B.B.A. and Ph.D., University of Georgia
OCCUPATION: United States senator
FAMILY: Two children by his first wife; three children by his current wife, economist Wendy Lee Gramm, former chairman of the U.S. Commodities Futures Trading Commission
QUOTE: "I want to finish the Reagan revolution. Washington makes too many decisions that should be left to the American family."

SENATOR PHIL GRAMM IS A THIRD-PARTY PRESIDENTIAL candidate who just happens to be running for the Republican Party nomination.

Gramm, fifty-two, doesn't fit in anywhere. Not in the good-old-boy roughhouse politics of his home state of Texas, not in the staid precincts of the Senate GOP hierarchy, and certainly not in the Democratic Party, from which he fled as a rebellious pro-Reagan congressman in 1983. As for the Christian fundamentalists whose morality he endorses, Gramm warns them bluntly he will go only so far with their agenda: "I'm running for President, not for

preacher." This odd-man-out estrangement from establishments suits Gramm just fine. It is both his greatest strength
and his most serious weakness. Political labels are just
flags of convenience to be changed when the need arises. It
is in the area of political ideas that Gramm stands fast,
unwilling to compromise on his faith in the free-market
system.

Many have been tempted to compare Senator Phil
Gramm with Barry Goldwater, that other maverick
Republican presidential hopeful, who took his party so far
over to the right in 1964 that it disappeared into oblivion
until Richard Nixon's comeback in 1968. Like Goldwater,
Gramm's drive for the nomination is a fight for the
Republican conservative soul—there is no temporizing in
Gramm's rhetoric, no compromise. His first political act as
an adult was to contribute $60 and his vote to Goldwater's
bid for President. Parodying the country-and-western hit,
Gramm tells his audiences, "I was conservative before conservative was cool," and he gets cheers in return.

But is America ready to be that cool? Gramm's problem
is that while he might be conservative enough to get nominated, he, like Goldwater before him, might be too stark a
contrast to the accommodating Clinton to get elected. Even
Republicans who lean more to the slow-talking former
Texas A&M economics professor than to traditionalist
rival Bob Dole know this. Publicly, and especially in
important early test appearances in New Hampshire (which
should be a Gramm "gimme"), there has been none of the
fervor that Goldwater generated more than thirty years ago.

True, Gramm has won his share of straw polls among
the GOP activists of various states (California, South
Carolina, Michigan, Missouri, Louisiana, and Arizona)
where his Georgia drawl with the veneer of a Texas twang
doesn't grate on the ear. But outside the deep South and
Far West, Gramm has trouble getting past a personal image

that one columnist described as "a sourpuss college professor with a yahoo drawl and the mean squint of a bill collector." Gramm quips in response, "I've never been able to get *anywhere* on my good looks and charm."

Charm is definitely a problem. Gramm is notoriously brusque when approached by tourists in the Capitol. He makes only perfunctory appearances at party fund-raisers, in contrast to front-runner Bob Dole, who tries to shake every hand in the house. His public scorn of some senior Republicans in both House and Senate has not endeared him to anyone.

Worse, despite being the first of the major candidates to begin his race–fully twenty months before the November 4, 1996, election—Gramm got off to a faltering start. Despite a massive fund-raising effort that may push him to the $47 million federal campaign spending limit before anyone else, Gramm was plagued for several months by the lack of a scheduling-and-issues team that had experience in running nationwide. As result, even though he has raised and spent two dollars for every one raised by both Dole and Lamar Alexander, he has not broken his tie for second place with the former Tennessee governor. He has since reshuffled his top advisory staff but is a long way from catching up with front-runner Dole.

More than is the case for any other candidate in the race, Phil Gramm's chances depend on his running a near-perfect race from now on. He does not have the margin of error that Dole enjoys. By staking out the strongest ideological position, Gramm is wagering on long odds. For him to win, the new political direction highlighted by the GOP's 1994 congressional sweep must continue to hold sway. Republican activists, and later American voters in general, must be willing to take a big risk on the radical reforms Gramm espouses. An unexpected turn of events— an abrupt hiccup in the economy or a frightening foreign crisis—could send his supporters scrambling for the comfort of the middle ground.

But William Phillip Gramm is no Goldwater. Setting aside the Arizona senator's hawkish views on the Vietnam War, Goldwater emphasized a stark, even draconian domestic economic policy that offered potential voters no positive vision of America's future. He stunned farmers by calling for an end to crop supports; he was booed by senior citizens when he threatened to cut Social Security benefits. His "extremism in defense of liberty is no vice" speech frightened blacks, Jews, and middle-class voters of all ethnic backgrounds. At base, Goldwater presented a harshly unsympathetic image of the American establishment, and most voters rejected both the man and the message.

Phil Gramm, on the other hand, belongs to no establishment at all. The vision he offers is the pleasantly familiar one of restoring to the American people the control over their values and destinies that many believe has been usurped by successive Washington administrations, both Democratic and Republican. His platform, however, is more specific (and therefore rigid) in its promise not only to reduce the size of the federal bureaucracy but also to eradicate named government agencies and functions ranging from the Department of Education to specific affirmative-action orders. What makes the GOP old guard unhappy is that this fixed purpose of Gramm's has often led him to clash openly with his team's respected leader, Senator Dole, as often as he has with the Clinton administration. Worse, Gramm has broken Ronald Reagan's unwritten law ("speak ill of no Republican") by blasting Dole for being too willing to make budget and welfare compromises with the hapless Democrats.

"I know who I am and what I believe in. When I stand up for what I believe in and it is not popular, I am not deterred," Gramm said in an early interview. But Gramm is convinced that his positions are popular where it counts, with the voter. "I believe the 1994 elections did represent a watershed decision by the American voter to change this country. I think it was the most dramatic election results since 1932, and it has the potential to reorder American politics for a half a century," he said.

"I believe the driving force behind the 1994 results was a growing concern among Americans that there were long-term, fundamental problems in the country that were not being addressed; that the American dream was endangered; and that government needed dramatic change," he explained. "For the first time in recent memory, pollsters are asking people, 'Do you believe your children will have a brighter future than you had?' And now, by a two-to-one margin, people say no; that's totally unprecedented. And I think we should have seen it coming in 1992, when 19 percent of the people voted for Ross Perot because they didn't believe that either of the two major political parties was addressing our problems. And they were right."

Gramm clearly relishes the role of odd man out; it fits his driven personality, and there is no doubt that up to now he has had great success bucking the prevailing tides. From the time he arrived in the House of Representatives in 1968, he clashed almost at once with the "go-along-to-get-along" leadership style of Democrats Jim Wright and Tip O'Neill. Gramm's style is modeled instead on head-on confrontation, and has been from the start of his political quest.

Gramm has been outside trying to bang his way to success for most of his life. He was born in 1942, the youngest of three children of a career Army sergeant based at Fort Benning, Georgia. When Gramm was five, the family's fortunes took a bad turn when his father suffered a stroke and thereafter spent his life as an invalid. Gramm's mother, who had only a seventh-grade education, had to go to work as a practical nurse for private patients in Columbus. By his own admission, young Phil was rebellious and a regular truant from school because of his inability to read. He failed the third, fifth, and seventh grades, and finally, at the age of fifteen (after he had been caught joyriding in his mother's car), Gramm was sent to a military school to shape up.

The discipline worked. Using scholarships available to the children of career soldiers, Gramm earned a B.A. and a Ph.D., both in economics, from the University of Georgia and then took a teaching post at Texas A&M, where he became a full professor in 1973. He also took on private business consultancies, wrote a flood of articles for professional journals and newspaper editorial pages, and dabbled in local real estate. His first marriage failed, but in 1970 he married Wendy Lee, a descendant of Korean immigrants, who boasted a more distinguished academic background (Wellesley and Northwestern) and who is in many ways a more conservative economist than her husband. The Gramms have two college-age sons. Mrs. Gramm has won her own career spurs serving as chairman of the Commodities Futures Trading Commission in both the Reagan and Bush administrations. She was dubbed "Ronald Reagan's favorite regulator" and has hotly rejected the notion that as First Lady she would be relegated to soft issues and ribbon-cutting ceremonies.

Gramm's first foray into politics was a disastrous lesson in fund-raising and campaign organization that he has never forgotten. In a 1976 challenge to incumbent Senator Lloyd Bentsen for the Democratic nomination, Gramm garnered only 2 percent of the vote. Two years later, when a House seat became vacant, Gramm was ready and was elected with 65 percent of the vote, increasing that margin to 95 percent in the two succeeding elections. A bumptious self-promoter from the start of his House career, Gramm quickly began to vex the Democrats who controlled Congress when he formed a partnership with a Republican congressman named David Stockman and began to embrace a conservative position on energy and economics issues. They retaliated by denying him a seat on the committee he coveted most, the House Budget Committee. But in 1981 the new House Speaker, Jim Wright, a fellow Texan, thought he had extracted a promise from Gramm to toe the party line more faithfully in exchange for the budget-committee posting.

Whatever Gramm had promised the Speaker (the two sharply disagree now on the conversation), Gramm quickly allied himself again with Stockman, who had shifted to the White House to be Ronald Reagan's master budget architect. While the Democratic leadership fumed, Gramm not only fed Stockman secrets from the budget committee's deliberations but also joined with a Republican congressman, Delbert Latta, to sponsor President Reagan's first budget bill. The Gramm-Latta Budget Act of 1981 and a tandem Reconciliation Act by the duo increased defense spending, slashed 250 social-program allocations, and mandated the tax cut that was Reagan's economic centerpiece. Together, the two bills cut federal domestic spending by $130 billion.

The Democrats took their revenge during the next session of Congress by expelling Gramm from the budget committee. He promptly resigned his House seat and ran as a Republican in a special election a few weeks later. Gramm became the first Republican elected from that district; he was back on the budget committee a few days later. In that term he voted with the Reagan Administration on more than two-thirds of the showdown roll calls, supporting the White House line on paramilitary aid in Nicaragua and El Salvador, voting against more Social Security benefits, expanded affirmative-action programs, and abortion funding, and voting for school prayer and freezing doctors' fees under Medicare.

When he won a bitterly contested U.S. Senate race in 1984, Gramm did not wait long to pursue his maverick course through the more sedate chamber. He teamed up with Senators Warren Rudman and Ernest Hollings, and the three sponsored an amendment to the 1985 debt-ceiling extension (then approaching $2 trillion) that set a mandatory deficit-reduction timetable that was supposed to lead to a balanced budget by 1991. The Gramm-Rudman-Hollings law was the first Congressional deficit measure with real teeth; it was designed to trigger across-the-board cuts in federal programs if the targeted goals were not met by Congress or the White House each year. In its first year of operation, 1986, the law cut $11.7 billion in domestic and defense spending to meet the $171.9 billion target. In later years, succeeding administrations found ways to bypass the law's mechanisms by skillful accounting fictions, including postponing spending authorizations and pushing up tax-revenue estimates. Still, the law proved that something could be done about runaway deficits.

The advent of Bill and Hillary Rodham Clinton provided Gramm with his most rewarding chance yet to set himself up as a formidable force in opposition to both the reaching plans of the new-style Democrats in the White House and the holding action of the Senate's Republican old guard. While Senator Dole and other leaders were cautious in their opposition to the Clinton agenda—from protecting gays in the military to the omnibus health-care proposals— Gramm showed a genius for first staking out the most aggressive opposition stance and then getting other Republicans (and quite a few apostate Democrats) to go along. The Clinton health plan, he said, "will pass over my cold, dead political body." And he made the threat stick.

True to form, late in 1993 Gramm began making

detailed plans to run for the presidency. In addition to employing the latest techniques in fund-raising from individual contributors, Gramm began to lay out a policy program that probably is the most detailed and firmly stated of any of the candidates' platforms. It is clear that the battleground of the 1996 elections will be the size and shape of the federal government, and Gramm has commented on what the Washington establishment would look like after his time in the White House. "Smaller," he said in an interview. "I don't think you can perform miracles in four or even eight years. But the government would be smaller. Working people would keep more of what they earned. We currently spend about 22.5 percent of gross national product, and we tax about 19 percent of gross national product. Our first goal, then, ought to be to get spending back down to the 19 percent level. Then I would start a second wave where you would cut taxes and cut spending on areas that were basically either things families could do better for themselves if you let them keep the income, or that state and local governments should be carrying out, not the federal government. Let them seize the taxing authority and fund the programs they want. By that road I think it would be possible to get the federal government down to 15 percent of gross national product, and I believe America would be richer, freer, and happier if we did."

A Gramm presidency also would radically change the economic landscape that America has grown used to over the last fifty years. "I would look at throwing out the income tax altogether. A broad-based consumption tax could tax a lot of income that is not being taxed. We could eliminate the intrusion by the IRS in our personal lives," Gramm said.

"As for a broad-based tax cut, I would not favor that. But what I want to do is transfer spending from the government to the family. One example would be to eliminate the

Department of Education, take the $32 billion a year we
spend, give half of it to parents through a $2,000-per-child
education tax deduction, give the other half to local school
boards, and let those locally elected members, parents, and
teachers set the priorities. I think it is time to admit that the
federal government can't do the job, but I don't call that a
tax cut."

Gramm would tinker with corporations' economic environment as well. He thinks it would be perfectly reason-
able to cut government subsidies by the same amount
needed to fund the capital-gains tax cut, cutting the capital-
gains tax rate each year by the same amount of economic
growth it spurs. When pressed as to which business subsidies he means, Gramm responded with a list that includes
government funds for overseas advertising of U.S. exports,
tax credits, farm subsidies, and even write-offs for all business entertainment. Estimates of savings range as high as
$167 billion a year, about three times as much as the $50 to
$60 billion he also wants to cut from such traditional
social-welfare programs as food stamps, children's aid
efforts, and housing subsidies for the poor.

On the other social issues that are part of the 1996 election-year checklist, Gramm opposes the anti-immigration
legislation ideas of rivals Governor Pete Wilson and Pat
Buchanan, although he has pledged to double the size of
the Border Patrol and increase funds for the FBI and Drug
Enforcement Agency in the war against drugs. He would,
by executive order, abolish President Clinton's industrial
policies and the various affirmative-action rules contained
in various federal regulations governing everything from
highway construction to broadcasting licensing. He
opposes raising the minimum wage and would be the first
President in recent memory to applaud the Federal
Reserve's tight money policies.

Can Gramm win? Charles Black, the top strategist of the

Gramm campaign, worked the numbers. "Since the whole primary campaign is compressed into February and March, by March 26, when the California primary is held, we will have the de facto nominee. After that, there won't be time to play catch-up." By the end of May, 70 percent of the GOP convention delegates will have been committed. But committed to whom? And what will Gramm's share be?

In the plus column, 55 percent of the Republican delegates will come from southern and western states. Many of these same states have winner-take-all primaries, so that if Gramm carries the vote, even by 51 percent to 49 percent, he gets all that state's delegates. In the Northeast and Midwest, where Dole is running strong, many primaries award delegates proportionally, so even if Gramm is trounced, he will still come out with some delegates. The Gramm strategy, according to Black, is based on the assumption that Dole will win the Iowa caucus on February 12 and the New Hampshire primary on February 20. The also-rans will then be narrowed to just Lamar Alexander and Pat Buchanan, behind Gramm. Arizona, with twice as many delegates as New Hampshire, must give Gramm his first big win, and then he must sweep the southern crescent of states, such as Louisiana, Georgia, and South Carolina. While Dole might win New York's 102 delegates on March 7, Black gives Gramm most of the 400 delegates in March 12's Super Tuesday spread of primaries (including Texas's 123 seats) and a clear lead. Black also reasons Gramm will pick up strength in California no matter what happens. With Pete Wilson out of the race, Gramm believes he can actually carry the state with its huge block of ultraconservative voters.

Still, even the Republican delegates may be faced with a choice that comes down not to the issues but to which candidate they like most. Can Gramm overcome his self-confessed harsh image? In response to such questions, Gramm tells of his dogged, and initially unsuccessful, courtship of Wendy Lee. "I make a poor first impression, I know that. But I do wear well once you get to know me—unlike that other fellow down the street. He makes a great first impression but loses ground after that."

<u>PRIORITIES</u>

1. Pass a balanced-budget amendment to the Constitution
2. Cut spending for most social-welfare programs
3. Abolish the Department of Education
4. Cut taxes for working families, including a direct payment equal to half the Department of Energy budget
5. Enact anti-abortion laws
6. Repeal gun control regulations
7. Repeal NAFTA treaty, GATT, and U.S. membership in the World Trade Organization
8. Put an end to U.N. control of U.S. troops abroad
9. Enact tougher crime laws and swifter capital punishment

TURNING BACK FROM THE BRINK

NAME: Colin Luther Powell

BORN: April 5, 1937

EDUCATION: B.A., City College of New York; M.B.A., George Washington University

OCCUPATION: Career soldier, beginning as second lieutenant and retiring in 1994 as Chairman of the Joint Chiefs of Staff

FAMILY: Married to Alma Vivian Powell; one son, two daughters

QUOTE: "I am not a candidate for President or for any other elected office in 1996."

NOT SINCE GENERAL WILLIAM TECUMSEH SHERMAN disappointed his supporters ("I will not accept if nominated and will not serve if elected.") at the 1884 Republican National Convention have there been so many political experts who guessed wrong about the political ambitions of a military hero.

In the end, after an energetic whistle-stop campaign disguised as a national book promotion tour, General Colin Powell shrank from actually entering the lists as an announced candidate for the GOP 1996 nomination. And who could blame him? A private man after a life of arduous military service and personal sacrifice (not to mention a wife with chronic health problems), Powell has since dropping out confided to friends he sometimes wondered how he got involved in Presidential politics after he retired as Chairman of the Joint Chiefs of Staff in 1994.

There is an answer to his wondering. And that answer also explains why, despite having explicitly abandoned elective politics for 1996, it also is possible that Colin Powell may return to the fray at some later date. The answer, simply put, is that Colin Powell would like *very much* to be President of the United States. However, he is not ready for, as he described it, "the down and dirty" of actually running for the job.

This is not the last of the Colin Powell phenomenon in American politics by any means. If there is a Republican elected to the White House in 1996, some sort of senior Cabinet post is possible. Moreover, there is the history of General Dwight D. Eisenhower to remember. The nonpartisan Eisenhower turned down an exploratory bid from the Democrats in 1948 which would have President Harry Truman stand down in his favor. Ike assumed that Republican standard bearer Thomas Dewey, whom he liked very much, would defeat Truman's bid for election that year and was moved by fear in 1952 that Truman was considering a second election bid and so entered the race himself. So it is possible that Powell may yet enter the lists for the White House in some future election.

Having said that, while Powell has taken himself out of contention for 1996, his specter looms large over the other candidates—those of both parties—who remain in the race or on the edge of the sidelines. Without intending to, Powell's tentative exploration of making a run, and his subsequent withdrawal, have had two immediate short-run impacts on the current race. He has exposed the lackluster aura that surrounds those who lead the pack among the GOP contenders for that party's nomination. So the immediate beneficiaries are, one, President Bill Clinton, whose chances for reelection have been greatly enhanced without Powell in the race. Two, there are the middle-of-the-pack Republicans, Senator Dick Lugar and ex-Governor Lamar Alexander chiefly, who will now get closer attention from GOP primary selectors who worry about Senator Bob Dole's chances and don't want further right alternatives of the Senator Phil Gramm–Pat Buchanan flavor.

This latter impact is made plausible by the very reasons that made the Powell candidacy so tantalizingly attractive in the first place. The same dynamics that made Powell viable now have been inherited by Alexander and Lugar (and House Speaker Newt Gingrich, when he makes up his mind). The key is simple: stop Bob Dole from winning a first-ballot victory at the San Diego nomination convention; a moderate who unseats Dole then becomes a genuine competitor to dump Clinton in November. A brokered GOP convention is essential and the outcome of the California primary on March 26 is the key to whether Powell can arrive in San Diego having denied Bob Dole enough delegates for a first ballot nomination.

The very delegate strategy which might have worked for Powell could work the same way for another Dole opponent. The number of delegates at the San Diego convention will be approximately 1,984, which means that the eventual nominee must capture 993 delegates to win. Dole's strength lies in the Midwestern and Northeastern states where selection rules most often award delegates to candidates on a proportional rather than winner-take-all basis. The so-called Powell strategy calls for a Dole challenger at the very least to run second to the senator in New Hampshire and to either win or split the delegations of those states (Maine, Connecticut, Vermont, Massachusetts, Rhode Island, Maryland, Georgia, and Colorado) which vote on March 5. Total delegates at issue: 224. On March 7, New

York puts its 102 delegates up for a vote. Then on March 12, "Super Tuesday" elections in Florida, Hawaii, Mississippi, Missouri, Oklahoma, Tennessee, Texas, and Washington auction off 399 delegates. On March 19, another 229 delegates are up for grabs in Illinois, Ohio, Michigan, and Wisconsin. In states such as Pennsylvania, Kentucky, and Michigan, proportional allocation is the rule and even a second-place winner can at least divide the pot there. In many of the southern states, including Phil Gramm's base of Texas, non-Republicans are able to vote in the primary, which means large concentrations of black voters could sweep key precincts across the region.

California's primary on March 26 with its 163 delegates thus becomes the linchpin to any prospects for a brokered convention. With Pete Wilson out of the race as well, a Dole challenger must prevail in California. Anyone but Dole in California if anyone else is to have a prayer of pre-vailing at the convention. By this rough calculus, Dole, still the front-runner, would arrive in San Diego with fewer than 700 delegates pledged to him, and that means no other candidate or candidates can swing enough of their votes to the senator to ensure first ballot triumph. If the viable chal-lenger can garner enough delegates to be in clear second place ahead of Gramm on the first ballot, then all bets are off, the delegates are free to nominate who they will. What makes all this at all plausible is the silent but growing fear deep in GOP bosoms that Senator Dole can't beat Bill Clinton and that some more moderate challenger must be found to pull enough of the swing voters from 1994 out of the Democratic alliance and push on to victory.

What has Powell supporters disappointed was that the general had what it takes to make the scenario a reality. By merely dangling the prospect that he might be interested, people of all colors showed they were ready to elect their first black President and that they were willing to invest a lot more trust in his leadership than they were in any of the current choices. Powell's people at the time argued the 1996 election had become a matter of "credentials and character." These are two traits that the general has in abundance. Powell is, of course, something more than a military hero, although he certainly is that. Two tours in Vietnam as a combat officer left him with eleven decorations and a Purple Heart. As the White House security successor to the ill-fated Admiral John Poindexter, General Powell is credited with reviving the National Security Staff in the Reagan administration and setting in place the safeguards that would prevent another such disastrous adventure as Irangate. As head of the Joint Chiefs, his finest hour came during the largely successful Desert Storm conflict and the subsequent restructuring of the Pentagon's capacity to move strike forces to single operation locations as part of an overall revision of U.S. defense strategy.

But Powell also boasts an M.B.A. from George Washington University and speaks the language of business as well as that of the soldier and strategist.

Powell is answering questions about himself through a self-searching autobiography that became an instant bestseller. The book, *My American Journey,* is a statement of what he believes in and how he addresses the major issues confronting the country. It also is one of the most carefully crafted political documents of this century. Most of Colin Powell's attitudes find him deliberately in the middle ground of American opinion. Even on the hot-button issues, Powell manages to be where most voters find themselves these days. More importantly, he stands where the majority of Republicans stand, regardless of the noise from the far right. He believes, he says, in what America believes. Sadly for his followers, he did not have enough desire for the struggle in this election. He is not out of American politics by any means. But he has let slip by a rare opportunity that comes to few enough other Americans. Will he be the Eisenhower of the year 2000 or the Sherman of 1884? That remains to be seen.

PRIORITIES

1. Prefers conservative fiscal policies but has a "social conscience"
2. Favors policies that encourage mothers to carry babies to term and put them up for adoption. "But if she decides she must have an abortion, that's her choice. So I'm pro-choice."
3. Favors gun ownership but wants registration and waiting periods
4. Wants to "reestablish moral standards" and end "ethnic fragmentation"

CAMPAIGN MONEY:
HOT BUTTONS AND SOFT DOLLARS

THE 1996 PRESIDENTIAL CAMPAIGN IS GOING TO BE nasty, expensive, and long.

There will be plenty of blame to go around. But by November 5, 1996, an exhausted and turned-off electorate will have endured the presidential campaign from hell, complete with a sordid scramble for unimaginably large sums of contributions, which will have paid for some of the most negative political commercials on record on behalf of a slate of candidates who share a general inability to inspire confidence.

How bad will it get? The coming campaign could spell the end of the two major political parties as they have existed since the Civil War. Do not be surprised if *several* third-party candidates emerge in the late spring in response to a general revolt among independent voters (who may account for more than one-third of the electorate this time). The hope of the non-party runners is at least to become major players in the ultimate selection process if the final choice collapses into the U.S. House of Representatives. And don't be surprised if some of the independent candidates are renegades from either the Democratic or Republican ranks who felt betrayed by the party machine's ability to turn off the flow of campaign funds and to deny them their chance to speak to the issues.

"Hell, the two political parties *are* the problem," snorts Lowell Weicker, the former governor of Connecticut who is mulling a plague-on-both-your-houses campaign for President that will aim at the disenchanted center of the voting population.

Michael Vlahos, a political analyst for the Progress and Freedom Foundation, notes that the Democrats are praying this will be a repeat of the 1948 come-from-behind election, which Truman won. The Republicans are for a sweep like that of Eisenhower in 1952. Indeed, if the past is any guide, the rule is that the candidate who raises the most money in either party's primary will win nomination and the nominee with the most funds through the summer will win the White House. Minimum price tag for the U.S. presidency? *At least* $44.7 million, according to most campaign consulting groups. But with the federal limit on individual contributions (called "hard money"), the total expenditure (counting "soft money") will probably top $100 million for each of the two major-party finalists. A losing candidate will have to pony up between $50 million and $75 million.

Hard money? Soft money? Welcome to the Alice-in-Wonderland world of campaign financing.

For nearly twenty years, post-Watergate reformers have tried to limit the impact of special-interest groups and their ability to deliver huge sums of contributions to political candidates. Thus there are limits on hard money—funds given by individuals, unions, and corporations to the candidates for the various federal offices up for election. As a lure for compliance, the federal government gives matching funds (an amount of tax dollars equivalent to the amount raised) to candidates who agree to abide by the restrictions.

As an unintended result of these restraints, big-dollar contributors have rushed through a loophole marked "soft dollars." These are funds given directly to political parties or to specific educational foundations in order to help inform the voters on the issues and to promote voter enthusiasm where it is lagging. In theory, the candidates do not benefit from these funds, but of course they do.

Take Bob Dole's Better America Foundation, which raised more than $4.6 million from a celebrity-studded list of corporate CEOs and financiers who ponied up between $15,000 and $250,000 each to help the senator make known his agenda without technically advocating his candidacy for office. Of course, it helped that Dole's picture graced most of the foundation's printed material and that the candidate was the central figure in a television commercial produced by the group. Among the big-name donors to the foundation was financier Ronald Perelman, whose contribution of $250,000 was the largest. Then there was Robert E. Allen, of AT&T, the communications giant ($100,000); Dwayne Andreas of the Archer-Daniels-Midland agricultural chemicals producer ($50,000); Stephen Bechtel, Jr., heir to the engineering firm ($25,000); Wayne Calloway, of PepsiCo ($10,000); Peter Coors, of the brewery family ($25,000); investors Theodore Forstmann ($50,000); John Kluge ($100,000); and Carl Lindner ($100,000). Also contributing were oilman T. Boone Pickens, who was Dole's campaign-finance director ($100,000); John Snow, of CSX Corporation, the transportation conglomerate ($100,000); and Jack Welch, of General Electric ($25,000). When there were complaints recently that the foundation skated too close to the boundary between hard and soft money, Dole shut it down and said the $2.6 million that was unspent would be returned to the donors.

But the donors, and a host of other regular big-dollar
contributors, won't be holding on to the funds for long.
Dole's foundation contributors will find a way to get the
money to their candidate somehow. They will be helped
and encouraged by other well-known Dole contribution
providers, including financiers Henry Kravis; Donald
Marron, of PaineWebber; Donald Trump; and James
Cayne, of Bear, Stearns. Dole's rival Phil Gramm can
boast former treasury secretary William Simon on his
money-raising team, along with bankers Thomas Rhodes,
former Goldman-Sachs chief; Harvey Golub, of American
Express; and Chemical Bank's Walter Shipley. Lamar
Alexander's team includes John Henessy, of CS First
Boston; Peter Flanigan, of Dillon Read; James Robinson
III, the former American Express chief; and William
Schreyer, formerly of Merrill Lynch.

Of course, some big-dollar contributors give "soft dollar"
money to both parties' national committees and other foundations through their political action committees (PACs).
Here the scene is more confused and volatile than ever.
Over the past twenty years, those who double-doled their
political dollars had fallen into the habit of giving the
Democratic National Committee (DNC) and Democratic
candidates generally more money than they allocated to the
GOP. But that was until it became painfully obvious last
autumn that the Republicans were surging back into power.
Then a very inelegant rush to the side of the winners took
place.

According to data filed with the Federal Elections
Commission, the Democrats' soft cash flow during the
period between January 1993 and the end of September
1994 saw them pull in $35.1 million, to $27.5 million for
the Republicans. In the crucial weeks between October 1,
1994, and the end of November, there was a surge of
money to the GOP committees: $16.2 million to the

Democrats' $4 million. The trend continued through the end of 1994, with the Republican National Committee (RNC) garnering a total for the year of $45.4 million, compared to $39.9 million for the DNC–a gain of $17.9 million for the Republicans versus an increase of only $4.8 million for the Democrats.

Not all the double-dolers guessed right. American Financial Corporation gave $525,000 in soft dollars to the DNC and $430,000 to the RNC. Archer-Daniels-Midland tilted the wrong way, too, with $481,000 to the DNC and $345,000 to the RNC. The big losers were Beneficial Corporation, which gave $397,250 to the Democrats against $86,500 to the GOP, and the Mashantucket Pequot Tribe, which gave $365,000 to the DNC and just $100,000 to the RNC. Smart guys at Atlantic Richfield gave $443,000 to the Republicans and $274,000 to the DNC, while executives at RJR Nabisco did even better, contributing $422,252 to the RNC and just $107,650 to the Democrats.

But while the Republicans enjoyed this financial advantage into the early weeks of 1995, the tremendous power of an incumbent President has made Bill Clinton a bigger draw than the RNC. The latest Federal Elections Commission data show that the RNC raised a record $7.8 million in the first quarter of 1995, more than ten times what the party had been able to raise in the same quarter of 1993, the previous off-year period. Among the leading contributors were Philip Morris, GTech Corporation, Massachusetts Mutual Life, Pfizer, U.S. Surgical, the Distilled Spirits Council, and RJR Nabisco. But the reelection campaign of President Clinton and Vice President Gore has raised $9.4 million in that same six months and spent $3.3 million of it already on a highly successful television ad campaign that stressed the White House's tough stand on crime. While it could still do so, the DNC made good use of fund-raising events tied to big-ticket givers—$100,000 got you dinner with Bill and Hillary in the State Dining Room, while for just $1,000 you could come to the White House and shake Hillary's hand. An embarrassing press outcry about the custom has caused the Clinton team to abandon their fat-cat fetes. As with the RNC, spokespersons for the DNC stress the importance of telemarketing and mass-mail solicitations. Ninety-three thousand people have given to the DNC, and most contributions are $100 or less.

It is fair to point out that the comparisons may not be that good. Loyal Democrats really have only one place to send their money right now—to the White House. Republicans, however, are being pulled at least nine different ways. Setting aside the money sent to the national committee, the war chests of the top Republican challengers are comfortably full. Late data indicate that Bob Dole nearly equaled the Clinton haul through June 30, 1995, raising $9.3 million and spending $5.2 million, according to the Federal Elections Commission. Phil Gramm has $7.3 million on hand, while Dick Lugar has raised $2.5 million and spent $1.8 million. Trailing the pack is Robert Dornan, who laments that he has only $5,463 in campaign funds and may be pushed out of the running as a result.

Another important point to remember is that not all money raised by the national committees goes just for the presidential nominees. Vast sums must be allocated for the House and Senate seats that will be contested next year, and the costs of a congressional seat are proportionally just as expensive as winning the White House. In the 1994 GOP sweep of the Congress, the least amount of money spent by a candidate was $200,000, for a two-year House seat. The average price was actually quite a bit higher. Many winners had to raise treasuries of more than $1 million; the mean cost of a House seat was $570,000, while if the candidate challenged an incumbent, the cost averaged $625,000.

Political action committee money was an essential ingredient of most of these races. Again, the money was not always wisely spent. Thirty-four of the successful GOP challengers got an average of $81,850 in PAC money for their winning bids. But the thirty-four losing Democrats got three times as much PAC support, according to a survey by the National Association of Business and Political Action Committees.

Two other trends will loom large in Campaign '96. One is the self-financing wealthy candidate. The best-known of these are Ross Perot, who spent about $30 million of his own money for his 1992 race, and Michael Huffington, who paid $2 million out of his own pocket for last year's losing bid for a U.S. Senate seat. Unnoticed last year was the fact that thirteen of the freshmen congressmen contributed $100,000 or more to their own House campaigns. The most expensive seat went to Enid Waldholtz (R-Utah), who spent $1.6 million of her own money in her winning campaign.

Among the top PACs not affiliated with corporations were the American Federation of State, County, and Municipal Employees; the National Education Association; the Laborers' International Union; the National Rifle Association; and a host of health-care groups, food and beverage concerns, and trade-related organizations.

The other trend worth noting is the growing dependency of candidates on companies that have closely targeted lists of people who can be counted on to respond to direct-mail or telemarketing solicitation, making small to medium-size contributions. Does it work? Ask Oliver North, the current king of direct-mail fund-raising. In North's failed campaign for the Virginia Senate seat held by Chuck Robb, his campaign raised $20.3 million via a direct-mail and telemarketing campaign in all fifty states. Of that, $16 million came from direct mailings to 245,000 individual givers.

Officials at the Republican National Committee argue that mass-marketed fund-raising efforts offer proof that soft dollars can be raised without relying overmuch on big PAC contributions. Says Mary Crawford, an RNC spokesman, "More than 260,000 contributions were made to us in just January and February in amounts of less than $100. Of that, we got money from 85,000 people who said they have never given before."

Clearly voters are heated up to an extent not seen recently in American politics. That is not necessarily good news for the two major parties, but it does argue that the electorate is at least paying attention to the issues that bother them. These topics, though, are not necessarily the same issues being served up by the politicians.

Consider how the Democrats missed the boat in 1994. Democratic pollster Frederick Yang believes that "the most fundamental mistake the Democrats made after 1992 was believing that *change* is a noun, not a verb. Running on change is not enough. The voters felt they had given the Democrats the keys to the car and expected to go places. The results of the 1994 elections clearly show the voters' belief that the country hasn't gone anywhere."

Nor can the Republicans count too much on the Gingrich-led Contract with America to carry the day this year. Polls taken after the 1994 congressional races showed that voters were only dimly aware of the Contract's promises and were skeptical.

What did motivate voters was a number of issues that were not always clearly defined by the candidates and certainly were not dominated by the two parties. Candidates and their campaign managers are in a frantic search for hot-button issues that will seize the voters' imagination and cause anger, fear, and a commitment to vote a certain way. Immigration restrictions, school lunches for poor children, and the threatened rollback of affirmative action join gun control, crime, and abortion rights as issues that jerk the voter to attention, even though the debates about them may not inform or elevate. Not surprisingly, voters are frustrated and angry; they also are ambivalent about the ability of either party to solve problems. According to exit polling conducted by Mitofski International for a consortium of networks and newspapers, voters in 1994 were far more concerned about crime than any other issue, with 38 percent saying it was a major factor for them; interestingly, the Democrats squeezed ahead as the party believed best qualified to lead on that issue. Then came an issue called "economy/jobs," which was the motivator for 27 percent of the voters; again, the Democrats were judged superior. After that came taxes (22 percent); family values/morality (22 percent), abortion (12 percent), and foreign trade/NAFTA (just 2 percent), all of which the Republicans dominated. The Democrats also were judged better at solving problems related to health care (22 percent), education (18 percent), and campaign-finance reform (4 percent).

These figures hardly provide a mandate for either party. It may be that a clearer picture of who the voters are and what motivates them may emerge through looking at them by age, education, and other factors.

More women voted in 1994 than men, and the sexes were split on party preference by the same ratio, with 54 percent of women voting for Democratic candidates while 54 percent of men voting Republican. Young voters (ages 18–24) were heavily pro-Democratic, but voters 25 to 29 were less so, and succeeding cohorts edged more into the Republican ranks as they moved through the crucial 30-to-69 age groups. The same trend could be observed by educational groups. Voters with less than a high-school education were pro-Democratic by a two-to-one margin. The more education (on through graduate school) after that brought a more conservative affiliation, with one clear exception. The group known as "Some College"—consisting of people who had not finished four years of courses—had swung from being pro-Democratic in 1992 to being pro-Republican in 1994, by 53 percent to 47 percent. Pollsters consider this group, which has a high percentage of single women, to be the most volatile voting segment.

More attention needs to be paid, too, to the special-interest associations, most notably the Christian Coalition, Ross Perot's United We Stand America (USWA), and groups such as the National Rifle Association. Although none of these groups is publicly supporting any candidate or party, their members are heavily predisposed to Republican candidates. The big surprise in 1994 was the NRA, which can claim that 15 percent of those who voted in the last election were its members, against 9.6 percent who are members of the Christian Coalition and USWA's 6.7 percent share of the electorate. Traditionally the NRA used to back an equal number of Democratic and Republican candidates, but in 1994 it swung sharply and aggressively into campaigns on behalf of targeted GOP candidates with a success that earned it a grudging respect among other special interests, such as unions, environmental groups, and other PAC promoters.

The bottom line, then, is this: If the voters don't have their minds made up now, when are they going to get a chance to figure out what's important and which candidate can do the job?

Don't look to the primary system to be of much help. In order to attract the kind of media attention that will in turn excite the voters and draw big-name politicians to campaign in their states, the 1996 primaries will be earlier than ever. That compresses the actual time voters have to look the candidates over and to debate the issues. It also means that candidates will have to front-load their spending budgets to garner big wins in the earliest contests. By April 2, fully 62 percent of the delegates to the two major-party conventions will be chosen, and the front-runners could have it locked up by then. To confuse matters further, some state party organizations hold early caucuses to select some delegates and hold primaries later to select the rest of the group. Many states are still jockeying to schedule earlier—and, they hope, more exciting—primaries. As it stands, key tentative dates to watch are February 12 and 20, when the Iowa caucus and the New Hampshire primary, respectively, traditionally kick off the official campaign season, and two mega-batches of primaries on March 5 and on March 12, the date known as Super Tuesday. On March 26 the California primary offers the last major bloc of make-or-break votes for the candidates.

By compressing the time frame and forcing the media to hasten their interpretations of who won and who lost, most candidates for the GOP nomination (and any Democratic challenger to President Clinton) will have to either make significant showings in the earliest of the contests or forget about it. This is dangerous ground, for the early primaries have a tradition of tripping up front-runners and elevating also-rans to front-rank status, even when they officially lose.

Remember that it was not leaders Barry Goldwater or Nelson Rockefeller who triumphed in New Hampshire in the GOP primary in 1964—it was Henry Cabot Lodge. Eugene McCarthy polled a third of the votes in losing to Lyndon Johnson four years later but was judged to have triumphed. George McGovern was given a lease on life against Edmund Muskie four years after that. Gary Hart actually beat Walter Mondale in New Hampshire in 1984, and Pat Buchanan lofted himself into power-broker status in 1992 with just 37 percent of the vote. The same dynamics will come into play in Iowa in 1996. Bob Dole should have his neighboring state sewn up, and so there the contest will be to see how strong the second-place rival turns out to be. Both Gramm and Alexander must come in second in Iowa, while the two of them must do very well against not only Dole but also Buchanan and the rest of the pack eight days later, in New Hampshire.

That means more intense television blitzes, more brutally negative campaigning, and probably less attention to what is really bothering the voters. It will not be a pretty sight.

ALEXANDER'S RAG-TAG BAND

NAME: Andrew Lamar Alexander, Jr.
BORN: July 3, 1940
EDUCATION: B.A., Vanderbilt University; J.D., New York
      University
OCCUPATION: Lawyer
FAMILY: Married to Leslie "Honey" Buhler Alexander;
      four children
QUOTE: "I think our most effective foreign aid over the
      last half century has been our graduate programs
      at American universities attracting students from
      all over the world."

WITH HIS LONG LEGS STRETCHED OUT FROM HIS FIRST-class seat to the bulkhead on an Atlanta–New York flight, Alexander's mood and body were relaxed. The previous night, it had been Atlanta; this night, New York; the next day, Baltimore. The day after that, it would be Knoxville, or was it Nashville?

Lacking in self-confidence the lanky fifty-five-year-old is not; what he is still missing is national name recognition.

It was the spring of 1995. At the press conference he held at the Waldorf-Astoria hotel, Alexander asked New Yorkers to remember the Alexander name if Senator Bob Dole, the favorite in New York, starts to slip. But the illusion of Republican solidarity was just a facade for the press. Less than a month later, when Dole chastised

Hollywood for contributing to America's moral decline, Alexander was quick to nip at Dole's heels for not stating that Washington had a big hand in the moral crisis. Later still, in a National Press Club address, Alexander took another shot at Dole: "We've had twenty United States senators who've run for the presidency since 1976, and none of them has ever been elected." The Tennessee governor is hoping that Dole's age will play against him or that Dole will otherwise slip from his perch.

If Dole does falter, the Democrats would rather face Gramm than Alexander. One Democratic insider said, "If it's Lamar, he could run a very tough race," and he ticked off on his fingers the reasons: Alexander is a former governor of Tennessee, is a former president of the University of Tennessee, is a successful businessman, hails from a state on the border between North and South, and has no skeletons in the closet. "Lamar's a character people can trust— that's a tremendous advantage," said the Democrat.

Andrew Lamar Alexander was born July 3, 1940, in Maryville, Tennessee, in a Congressional district that has never sent a Democrat to Congress. He tells a story—possibly apocryphal—of a nearby town in the hills where civic leaders, in order to explain to children what a Democrat was, would parade any of the town drunks who happened to be incarcerated.

Alexander has been a lawyer; legislative assistant (to Tennessee senator Howard Baker, who subsequently became Alexander's political mentor and backer); governor of Tennessee; chairman of the Republican Exchange Satellite Network. The satellite and cable TV network organized three thousand Republican meeting sites in six hundred cities to help Republicans decide what they are for, commmunity by community. Alexander hosted nineteen of these Republican Neighborhood meetings, which got his name before big-time Republican donors. He is a fellow of the Hudson Institute, a conservative think tank. He has served as counsel to Baker's law firm, and he apparently owes much to his Baker connections, including several profitable corporate directorships and a couple of successful business ventures in which his own financial risk was minimal. He was also secretary of education in the Bush administration—but now he is advocating abolishing that post and the entire Department of Education.

Alexander plays at a form of Reaganism, favoring the shifting of decision-making from the federal government back to states and communities. He has an economic and political theme song to match, urging the creation of jobs by means of a fairer, simpler federal income tax, cutting the capital-gains tax in half, deregulation, and radical changes in education (he says that in 1981 he urged President Reagan to transfer funding and control for elementary and secondary education out of Washington). He is against a national sales tax, which he says undermines state and local strength. Indeed, Alexander boasts that during his two terms as Tennessee's governor, his state produced new jobs at twice the national average, went from last place to third place in the production of new automobiles and from forty-eighth to thirty-sixth in average family income, and enacted the nation's only state program to pay teachers more for teaching well. When he left office in 1986, Alexander said, the state government had fewer employees and a smaller debt than when he had arrived, and the state had the nation's fifth-lowest tax rate.

While he favors a strong, effective central government, he does not believe that it requires a full-time Congress. Alexander would reduce the pay of members of Congress and would send them home to their districts for half the year, to let them continue in their normal jobs as ranchers, lawyers, teachers, and business owners. Alexander favors paying all their expenses, but would require them to disclose fully all their outside income. This would counter corruption, he argues, and would cut down on the inside-the-Beltway mentality, which stems from the fact that once politicians arrive in Washington, they tend to talk only to one another.

On the hot topic of welfare reform, Alexander likes Senator Nancy Kassebaum's idea of swapping Medicaid for welfare. In other words, Alexander favors taking $55 billion of Washington-based welfare programs—Aid to Families with Dependent Children (AFDC), food stamps, and the Women, Infants, and Children (WIC) nutrition program—and giving that money all back to the states. "Bring all Medicaid back to Washington as step one to get it under control," he said, "then block-grant the entire Medicaid program back to the states."

Socially, Alexander characterizes his views as pro-life but says that he does not favor overturning Roe v. Wade. He says he is a supporter of civil rights and points to his support, as Tennessee's governor, for the Martin Luther King, Jr., holiday. But he opposes affirmative action: "I believe it's wrong to discriminate in favor of somebody based on race. I believe scholarships should be based on income to aid the middle class and the poor."

Alexander notes that Americans seem to be losing their confidence in the future and in their ability to affect that future. In April 1995 he told a National Press Club audience that "the promise of American life is this irrational belief in our unlimited future and that every one of us has an opportunity to participate in it." But, he told the group, during a cross-country drive the previous summer he had asked people to look ahead twenty years. Would their children and grandchildren have more opportunity than they themselves had? "I found most Americans afraid to say yes," he concluded.

In a book that he edited with Chester E. Finn, Jr., *The New Promise of American Life,* Alexander stresses that what America needs is "a future that discards many of the assumptions that ordered our lives in the twentieth century and replaces them with convictions grounded in the best of our traditions and suited to our highest aspirations for tomorrow." He insists that the American dream must be revived for those who no longer have hope, and that government in general, and the federal government in particular, places more obstacles in the way of that hope than it clears away. Alexander attacks the "arrogant empire" that is the federal government, and would replace its centralizing, uniform, monopolistic, no-fault approach with decentralization, diversity, and privatization.

While some of Alexander's positions smack of Reaganism and others of Nixonian Republicanism, a few of Alexander's views are off the beaten track. He's not exactly your standard politician, either. In 1978, he walked 1,000 miles across Tennessee in his quest to become its governor. After his two terms, the Alexanders moved to Australia for a half-year (during which time Alexander wrote a book, *Six Months Off*) not only to introduce their four children to another culture but also to get them adjusted to a normal family life after eight years of life in a fully staffed governor's mansion. And what makes a Lamar Alexander fundraiser or campaign stop different from most is the fact that he has a grand piano on stage and that he invariably sings a couple of anti-Clinton parodies, finishing up with, "Come on along . . . it's Alexander's ragtime band."

But Alexander insists that he has what it takes to be chief executive. "The skill you need most as President, as commander-in-chief, is executive decision-making," said Alexander during an interview. "It's one thing to give a running commentary on what's going on in Bosnia or somewhere, something else to execute plans to deal with it. I've had those executive decision-making skills as governor, as university president and cabinet member."

He points to his effectiveness as governor. "I was a

pro-growth governor and I would be a pro-growth president. I know what that means. If all I had done was balance eight state budgets [as required by Tennessee law],
we'd still rank forty-eighth in family income. We had no
capital in Tennessee. We were capital-poor, job-poor,
income-poor, education-poor. And our strategy was not to
try to regulate ourselves out of that but to create an
environment that was attractive to new capital and
entrepreneurs and to job creation."

He lured automakers such as Nissan and GM to
Tennessee, making Tennessee an entrepreneurial hot spot.
But he found that jobs weren't enough—corporate relo-
caters wanted a strong educational system, too. And that
became an Alexander strategy: "Tennessee is the only state
to pay teachers more for teaching well," he says.

The bedrock of Alexander's domestic economic belief is
this jobs-and-education two-step: that job creation and constantly improving educational standards worked for
Tennessee, will work for the United States, and can make
the United States a winner in the economic brave new
world that lies ahead.

A similar attitude holds in Alexander's view of Japan—a
country he's visited fourteen times since 1978, a country
whose corporate leaders he's wooed. Alexander says that
Japan, with a standard of living below that of the United
States and not as well prepared as America to deal with its
aging population nor as capable of creating new jobs, has
"industry-government policy practices [that] don't look
nearly as effective as they did ten years ago. Japan is going
through the same thing that we've gone through in the last
few years, downsizing, becoming more productive, competing in a more international economy. But I think it will be
much more difficult for Japan than for the United States."

As President, Alexander would create an environment
"that is attractive to capital. In the first place, we have one

out of every five dollars, and most Americans would prefer to invest their money here if they could. Number two, it's safer here. Look at what's happened in Russia, Mexico, and most other countries. This is a more predictable society than most other places you can go. And three," he said, "we're still one of the best places in which to create a start-up company or to expand a growing company."

In fact, Alexander and his wife did just that, starting Corporate Child Care, Inc., in 1987 with little of their own money but several outside investors and a $100,000 loan. The Alexanders have taken no money out of the company yet. "Today CCCI has more than twelve hundred employees and has been in the *Inc.* magazine fast-growing list for the last three years," Alexander boasted politely at each campaign stop.

In order to get elected, of course, Alexander will have to overcome his lack of name recognition. The candidate hopes to buy himself out of voter oblivion with television advertising—hence his preoccupation throughout 1995 with fund-raising, and his decision to start running television commercials in New Hampshire and Iowa during the summer.

The name recognition, like the money, has to come early. Even if he won New Hampshire or Iowa, that victory would occur too late for him to raise the money he needs in order to set the television campaign in motion. In 1996, unlike other election years, some 60 to 70 percent of the delegates will be selected by April 2. The campaign television commercials have to be ready by then, and time-slot commitments need to be in place. Given money and television, Alexander believes, he can even capture California.

Alexander is disciplined, and he masks a certain uptightness with an assumed flannel-shirt folksiness. And he can be more winning one-on-one, working the crowds, than his reserved demeanor sometimes suggests. But to say that

Alexander is running against Washington as an outsider is
a campaign fib. Alexander was walking the Capitol corridors for Baker at age twenty-seven, and at thirty he became
executive assistant to Bryce Harlow at the White House
Congressional Liaison Office. He was in and out of
Washington as chairman of the National Governors
Association (1986), as chairman of President Reagan's
Commission on Americans Outdoors, and as Bush's secretary of education. "But then I went home," he counters.

Can he win? "Five years ago," says candidate
Alexander, "America thought we would have President
Cuomo. And President Clinton was at five percent." He
seems to relish the prospect of reaching the point in the
campaign when the politicking gets serious and the media
are on hand to broadcast the best barbs and bitterest asides.

Aside from the question of whether America finds his
positions attractive and inspiring, his political strengths may
well be his ability to wage a strong fight for publicity and
money, to master the very things that have kept some very
well known names from tossing their hat in the Republican
ring. Money and the fierce fray are what Alexander apparently is counting on to get him seen, heard, and elected.

PRIORITIES

1. Implement term limits
2. Institute a balanced federal budget
3. Send welfare back to the states
4. Pursue free-market health-care reform
5. Extend free-trade agreements in Europe, Asia,
   and Latin America
6. Improve relationships with old allies and
   strengthen relationships with Russia and China
7. Stop the free fall in defense spending

GOOD TUNE,
POOR TIMING?

NAME: Richard Green Lugar
BORN: April 4, 1932
EDUCATION: B.A., Denison University
OCCUPATION: United States senator
FAMILY: Married to Charlene Smeltzer; four children
QUOTE: "Even if they were philosopher-kings, people at the federal level would be hard-pressed to mandate a welfare system to fit all fifty states."

IF THE ISSUE WERE FOREIGN POLICY, REPUBLICAN Senator Richard Lugar would be the candidate to beat. It's not, and he isn't—though the four-term Indiana senator does not accept that scenario.

Even while saying the U.S. electorate is sophisticated enough to choose a foreign-policy expert as president, Lugar's attempt to lure domestic-issue voters is with an economic policy that boils down to three little words— "Scrap the IRS!"

On a New England outing last year, Lugar repeated this catchphrase before the New England Council in the plush Boston Harbor Hotel's John Foster Room. At a podium from which he could gaze out onto the harbor in which

John Foster had dumped tea to protest taxation more than two hundred years earlier, Lugar, sixty-three years old, was offering a presidency that would dump the federal income tax and replace it with a national retail sales tax, a consumption tax.

This is an idea so big that first-time listeners are either startled or stunned—though Lugar insists that after people "walk around it a few times," it makes sense. Lugar's economic theory—he credits the Cato Institute and several economists for his thinking—goes like this:

If the federal income tax is scrapped, Americans would take home more of their paycheck. A 17 percent consumption tax would encourage Americans to save that extra money instead of spending it. Their savings would boost investment, which in turn would translate into greater global competitiveness, not least because American goods would no longer carry the added cost of income tax built into their price and would therefore be cheaper for foreign consumers to purchase. Foreign economic policy, then, becomes a matter of making sure the export avenues are kept uncluttered so that competitive U.S. goods can enter every world market.

Such a surge in productivity would return the United States to the 5 percent annual growth rate that was characteristic of the nineteenth century, a rate double the 2.5 percent promoted by the inflation-fearing Federal Reserve Board and U.S. Treasury.

Lugar would turn the states into consumption-tax collectors on behalf of the federal government. Poor people, both working and nonworking, and the middle-class would be protected either by an exemption from the first $5,000 of consumption taxes (which would take the form of a rebate check) or by the exemption of certain categories of purchases (food, medicines, maybe clothing and rent) from the consumption tax. The five billion man-hours needed

nationwide annually for compliance with the Internal
Revenue Service's rules—equal, says Lugar, to Indiana's
annual manpowerage—and the $5 billion to $7 billion paid
to the 150,000 people administering the tax code also
would be saved.

If Presidential politics came down to picking a decent man
from the Senate with big-city mayoral experience, former
Indianapolis mayor Lugar—a fiscal conservative known as
"Richard Nixon's favorite mayor"—would have an edge.
But mayors are out and governors are in. Republican governors, who control all the big states except for Florida, are
the new Republican kingmakers. Within the pack of contenders for the nomination, they know Lamar Alexander
because he chaired their association; they know Clinton,
who chaired it, too.

Within this group, Lugar's name pops up but doesn't
stay up. He was mentioned as an alternative among those
urging Perot to run in 1992. A fifth-generation Hoosier,
Lugar, an Eagle Scout who enlisted in the U.S. Navy in
1956 while a Rhodes scholar in London, is a farmer who
also has an interest in the family food-machinery firm
founded by his maternal grandfather and managed by his
brother, Tom.

Elected to the U.S. Senate in 1976 after two terms as
mayor, Lugar has chaired the Senate Foreign Relations
Committee and now chairs the Senate Agricultural
Committee. In 1994 he was reelected with 68 percent of
the popular vote. Over the years he has returned to the
Senate more than $2.4 million in unspent office funds.

Lugar's scrap-the-IRS pitch has been going around the
track for some time. House Ways and Means Committee
chairman Bill Archer was trotting it along congressional
corridors in late 1994. *Parade* magazine, a supplement to

many Sunday newspapers, has carried a couple of stories on it, and forty thousand readers wrote back saying they liked the idea. But even Lugar admits that his no-income-tax proposal takes some time to get used to.

While Lugar regards the abolition of income tax as his priority, he does not favor cuts in other taxes. The trim, intense senator considers balancing the budget to be the most desperate of the myriad "gnawing problems" facing the nation. He believes a balanced budget could be accomplished in seven years, provided it could surmount presidential veto threats.

"You see," he says, "even after we have mandated the committees, including my own in agriculture, to do certain things, if the President says, 'I don't want the American people to undergo the pain and difficulty of these arbitrary sacrifices, I'm going to veto the whole thing,' we're back to square one." Lugar thinks that it may take a Republican President to carry out such a measure. "But it must occur . . . [A President] has really got to be prepared to take the political heat to do it over a sustained period of time."

Lugar muses, as many candidates do, over the dilemma of Americans who want more time with their families or for their leisure activities, yet say they would work more hours if they could. "They feel they are not advancing," said Lugar.

He points out that in 1982, for example, when unemployment was high and industry was closing down, people's concern was simply getting back to work. Now economists can point to a recent period of economic growth, but, Lugar says, "many people say, 'But I'm still not sure that in real terms I'm getting there.' This is why I'm led to believe we really have to rearrange the taxation system—specifically the savings system that creates the investment pool we need to get the productivity gains, which, ultimately, alone can bring higher wages over a sustained period of time."

Despite the importance of his economic plan, Lugar recognizes that other issues preoccupy the American public as well. "My own view is that the Republican Party ought to be speaking to the problems of families' stability, to good parenting, to a supervision of adolescent males and females in our society. Passing crime bills and welfare bills may be [seen as a] public need but may not necessarily be effective—absent there being a more direct conversation [on personal responsibility] that a President ought to enter into with the people."

In September 1995 Lugar was one of the Republican hopefuls who attended the Christian Coalition conference in Washington, D.C. He sees the conservative evangelical group as "a very important part of a winning Republican coalition," and was at their conference seeking their support for a national prohibition against gambling. He was politely received by the audience, but by espousing this position he risks being pegged as the Carrie Nation of gambling and lotteries.

Another favorite Lugar topic is foreign policy. An essential complement to his domestic economic policy is a foreign economic policy that batters down barriers to American exports. He is against the Clinton administration's bailout of the Mexican economy, saying that he thinks the market could have worked there. At the 1995 World Pork Expo at the Iowa State Fairgrounds (which Lugar's rivals Bob Dole and Alan Keyes attended as well), he noted that for sixty years federal programs have been designed to suppress production rather than encourage it because "the thought was that if American agriculture were ever unleashed, we would produce so much we would have no idea what to do with it." The answer, according to Lugar, is greater exports.

His foreign policy has a noneconomic side as well. "The president of the United States is responsible for our foreign policy, for our security, as commander in chief, but beyond that he must be a hands-on manager of foreign relationships, strategic relationships that have to do with our security. This means Russia and China have to be a very important focus. It means building coalitions to fight terrorism and the proliferation of nuclear weapons."

Lugar is a reassuring and unflamboyant presence that people are happy to put themselves out for. He is a decent, responsible man—a credit to a discredited Congressional system. But his issues do not resonate. In the contest, he might not even carry his own state.

<u>PRIORITIES</u>

1. Balance the budget
2. Eliminate the income tax, which would lead to expanded trade opportunities
3. Review and eliminate unnecessary federal agencies, delegating more authority to the states, and implement regulatory reform
4. Implement a nonisolationist foreign policy, including controls on nuclear proliferation, containment of the Bosnia conflict, and strengthening and expansion of NATO
5. Eliminate the Department of Education and adopt a school-voucher system

REFUSING TO FLY?

NAME: Henry Ross Perot
BORN: June 27, 1930
EDUCATION: U.S. Naval Academy
OCCUPATION: Businessman
FAMILY: Married to Margo Perot; five children
QUOTE: "You can't tax people who aren't making money."

SET ALL JOKES, CARICATURES, AND CYNICISM ASIDE, and then look at Ross Perot.

What emerges is a single-minded, brusque martinet, a brilliant salesman who knows a great pitch when he hears it—and knows how to deliver one when he chooses to.

Single-minded? To a fault. Everyone knows the *On Wings of Eagles* story—the Ken Follett account of the daring, Perot-financed rescue of Perot's employees trapped in Ayatollah Khomeini's Iran.

But in the General Motors boardroom they tell the tale of Perot's briefcase. The scruffy holdall was resting on an antique buffet that had the usual breakfast-meeting offerings—fruit, muffins, water glasses—handsomely laid out on a starched linen-and-lace cloth. During the meeting, Perot was making a point and wanted to strengthen it. As he talked he reached behind him for the briefcase, and in sweeping it off the buffet he swept much else off besides. But he just kept on talking.

In 1992 Perot was a presidential candidate at the urging of others. That year he presented in a speech to the National Press Club his assessment of the state of the U.S. government: "The chief financial officer of a publicly owned corporation would be sent to prison if he kept books like our government. . . . All the personal income taxes collected west of the Mississippi are needed just to pay the interest on the national debt. . . . Maybe it was voodoo economics. Whatever it was, we are now in deep voodoo."

Perot hasn't changed his focus much in four years, though the General Agreement on Tariffs and Trade (GATT) has succeeded the North American Free Trade Agreement (NAFTA) and the U.S. bailout of the faltering Mexican economy on his hit list.

But four years ago, Perot permanently altered U.S. politics. His legacy is not just the United We Stand America (UWSA) organization, but the fact that the issues he espouses have become mainstream topics. Perot himself deals in encapsulated economics. He takes a theme, then wraps it in an example (or a non sequitur) to make his point. On the $4.8 trillion debt, for example: "Take every dollar bill, every five-dollar bill, every penny, nickel, and dime, and put them in one place, and it doesn't equal $4.8 trillion." On the trade deficit: "We have the largest trade deficit in the history of the world, but you don't hear that. The trade deficit is like cancer, [but we're] only willing to treat colds." On Social Security: "In 1950 we had sixteen people working [for each person on Social Security]. By 1990, three. In 2020, two. Here are the facts: The Social Security trust fund doesn't exist. We should have $500 billion accumulated in it, and all we have is a sheet of paper." On Mexico: "The White House and congressional leaders gave Mexico $20 billion of your hard-earned tax dollars [in a bailout], and the Mexican economy continues to fall apart." Bringing Mexico into NAFTA fueled Perot's ire in 1992. This time, GATT and the World Trade Organization (WTO) are the impetus behind his stated intention to create a third party.

In November 1994 Perot said that if Congress passed the GATT/WTO International Trade Agreement, he would start a third party. Perot argued that the legislation would result in $31 billion in lost revenues to the United States. Further, he contended, within the one-nation-one-vote World Trade Organization, the U.S. would lose its trade-decisions veto rights and U.S. laws could be overridden by the WTO.

"Eighty-point-seven percent of Americans rejected GATT," editorialized Perot, yet like NAFTA, the UWSA contended, "these issues are ignored by Congress because special interests and big business support tariff reduction as it affords them the opportunity to move manufacturing operations to low wage, underregulated countries while enjoying tax-free access to the huge U.S. consumer market."

On Sept. 25, 1995, on *Larry King Live,* Perot kept his word and said he would create a national Independence Party. In California, where such a party already exists, it would be known as the Reform Party, and steps were immediately begun to launch the party in that state.

While UWSA spokesperson Sharon Holman said the organization has never revealed its membership numbers, UWSA members in Iowa said that before the third party announcement, membership was just over one million and starting to decline. In the first five days after the announcement, nearly one million people called UWSA's toll-free number, which Perot displayed on *Larry King Live*.

Believe Perot on this: The peppy, pesky, fast-talking, doesn't-suffer-fools, won't-yield-an-inch, get-outta-my-way east Texan doesn't want to run for the presidency. And he doesn't have to in order to influence the race.

Said Joann Vinson, Maryland state UWSA chairman, "He has a rich and full life. Much about the presidency does not appeal to him, things some presidents like, like flying around in Air Force One. Perot would hate that—or the splendid isolation of the White House.

"True, he's got a magnetic charm and doesn't suffer fools gladly," added Vinson, who has known Perot since 1969, when she headed a cause dear to his heart—a league of families of soldiers missing in action (MIA) in the Vietnam War. "That's because he doesn't have time to waste, and he does focus on whatever it is like a laser beam."

Double billionaire Henry Ross Perot, sixty-five, made himself wealthy through his 1962 creation, Electronic Data Systems (EDS). This former IBM salesman sold EDS in 1979 to GM for $1 billion plus stock and a seat on GM's board. Boardroom unpleasantness led GM to buy Perot out, and he left to start Perot Systems. Four years later he spent an estimated $60 million on his 1992 campaign.

What Perot learned in 1991–92 was that he doesn't like the political process and isn't that keen on what a President has to do. He calls the media trials of a presidential bid "the attack-dog mess." He asks, "Is there anything in the world that anybody can allege about anybody that won't hit the front page?"

Perot threatens the Republicans more than he does the Democrats. In 1995 Newt Gingrich urged Perot not to run lest the 1996 election be thrown to President Clinton; candidate Lamar Alexander asked Perot to run, if he does put himself up as a candidate, as a Republican. And Perot himself is sensitive to charges that he put Clinton in the White House.

Meanwhile, UWSA, of which he is both talisman and leader, holds Perot's feet to the fire. He lured in those UWSA adherents and admirers, and they're holding him responsible as they found a third party and seek an independent presidential candidate.

Many Perot supporters speak of his sense of duty. But that sense seemingly creates a conflict within him, a conflict exacerbated by a billionaire's hubris. He is tantalized by a political process he detests. His Eagle Scout background and his Annapolis sense of duty make him feel as if he has to "protect" the electorate from the politicians; his success in life and the money at his disposal mean he has the wherewithal to do it.

But not the temperament.

Washington State UWSA chairman Connie Smith agrees that Perot would rather not run. "But he has always said he would do what's best," she commented, "for he is extremely concerned how voters are treated by elected officials."

In the past Perot personally reacted against what he saw as the United States' inability to alter world events—getting MIAs out of Vietnam, for example, or rescuing his employees from Iran. And while trying to make a difference on those very personal issues, he realized how unresponsive Congress and the White House actually were to the demands of the little man, even the extremely well-heeled little man. He was infuriated, and he still is. It was Perot's controlled fury on behalf of himself and others that finally spurred the 1992 bid.

For Perot, until the 1990s, personal considerations were always paramount to political considerations.

His populist and anti-party bid revealed that while at least 19 percent of the electorate voted for him, 40 percent of the people polled following the elections felt much as he did. Since then, Perot has remained a political presence, though when Iowans reported UWSA membership numbers down a little, it was possibly because there was no presidential candidate yet for them to rally behind.

As an independent presidential contender, Perot could enter the race quite late. In 1992 he was a sometimes-in, sometimes-out candidate, withdrawing from the campaign and reentering it again. In 1996 he could wait to see if there will be other third-party candidates—and he would have a fairly good idea who the leading Republican was. Perot's colleague Jim Squires has said that the mechanics of getting Perot on all fifty state ballots could be delayed until late in the spring of 1996.

Perot has been playing it canny. In October 1994 he launched a radio call-in show, which soon was broadcast on 160 stations. Among his guests were potential candidates for the Republican presidential nomination.

It was low-key, low-cost, and kept Perot in his self-defined presidential-broker role. When in June he canceled his own radio show, the UWSA newsletter nonetheless advised members how to present themselves on other people's call-in shows.

The long-planned August gathering that Perot organized in Dallas was intended to be a meeting of UWSA state chairmen, but it metamorphosed into a gathering that attracted most presidential candidates, though not President Clinton. Not since the 1984 Republican National Convention had so many White House aspirants been in the city at the same time. They were all allowed to give their pitch, while Perot, though the center of attraction, seemed oddly sidelined.

United We Stand America members who went to Dallas expecting to hear a definite yes or no from Perot were disappointed.

Since his 1992 bid Perot has sharpened his media skills—a bit—and has had lessons in on-camera techniques. On a talk show he can have the floor. He loves that. But he's wary of print journalists. Try to pin him down to answer a question or two in the VIP reception lounge before a National Press Club appearance, and he's uncommunicative. Send a faxed list of suggested questions, and he decides, "I can't be bothered with this stuff." Offer to fly out with him to a Michigan appearance, and the office never calls back. But give him the microphone, then hear him go. He is entertaining, sometimes funny, often apt—and a great source of quotable quotes.

Even so, with less than nine months to polling day, people still are asking: Where's Ross?

Can his Independence Party prosper?

Populist third parties in lively democracies generally always suffer the same fate. The two dominant parties help themselves to those third party planks that seem most useful. (That happened also in the Republican Contract with America, many elements of which parroted Perot.)

And Perot's creation of the Independence Party has not solved the major reason for which it was created—to field a presidential candidate. Who will it be? Perot wouldn't have minded backing Powell.

But since Powell bowed out, Perot's only high-profile alternative is himself. And while Perot could run, and run hard, Perot cannot win.

It's not just that Ross Perot doesn't want the White House. It's also that Perot's smart enough to understand he cannot get it.

PRIORITIES

1. Congressional term limits
2. Congressional ethics and lobbying reform

3. No tax increases without voter approval
4. A balanced budget amendment
5. Test Medicare, Medicaid, and Social Security program reforms. And once the results are understood, impose them nationwide

POLLS: VOTERS LOYAL TO ISSUES, NOT PARTY

EVERYTHING SEEMED SO CLEAR-CUT AFTER THE 1994 election results were in; the conservative tide, a veritable tsunami of ideological change, was triumphant. And some pollsters said, "We told you so."

But polls, politics, and statistics are one thing, people another. Individuals are not easily boxed into neat political categories.

Sociologist Bill D'Antonio offers the example of his own brother, a conservative who lives in Connecticut. According to the polls, that brother helped "throw the rascals out" in 1994. Yet that same kid brother—though he is a statistic in the conservative column—doesn't want his taxes cut. For the $140 he'd save, he'd rather keep the social programs that aid the needy.

That kind of attitude is not reflected in the polls. Conservatives are supposed to want to abolish taxes, period.

Do polls and surveys, stacking one group against another in the process of finding out what Americans think on every issue, in reality factor out the compromises, gray areas, and common sense of real life?

"The Numbers Are Far Too Often Wrong" runs the head-line of an article by Everett Carll Ladd in *The Public Perspective*, which is the journal of the Roper Center for Public Opinion Research and which Ladd edits. "Examined individually, the measures we increasingly live by," he writes, "range from excellent to simply awful." Yet, Ladd says, "social statistics have become a national necessity. Expectant, demanding, optimistic that problems can be solved, Americans want to know the answer to, 'How Are We Doing?'"

Explains D'Antonio, who is a professor of sociology at the Catholic University of America, in Washington, D.C.: Back in the early days of the Carter administration, polls on taxation showed "that 70-plus percent of the public then were in favor of raising taxes for a variety of things Congress is now talking about cutting."

Since President Ronald Reagan made taxation "a mortal sin," said D'Antonio, "people have been told their taxes are too high. But what's too high? It's a totally relative term. In Virginia they don't want a tax rebate if it means cutting into education."

Maybe it's not taxes people fear but the Internal Revenue Service and the IRS tax forms and threats of audits. But did anyone ask them that?

Do politicians, like pollsters and the rest of us, hear only what they want to believe? House Speaker Newt Gingrich told television interviewer Charlie Rose in July, "All we're saying is we believe this country wants a smaller govern-ment with lower taxes. We believe we have a mandate for that."

Gingrich is attracted to the work of the late industrial-organization specialist J. Edwards Deming, the American usually credited with being the father of Japan's economic miracle. Deming dealt with better organizing workers— Gingrich wonders aloud if industrial organizational methods could not be applied to society at large to make its members more productive.

According to Methodist theologian and corporate organization specialist David Trickett, however, the efficient organization of workers and the restructuring of corporations to meet productivity goals don't easily lend themselves to broader society. Further, adds Trickett, Deming, an active Episcopal layman, wrestled with himself during the last several years of his life, because he believed that he had unintentionally communicated a soulless understanding of human beings. He thought his transactional, process-oriented understanding of human beings had not conveyed such factors as the depth and complexity of individual hopes and aspirations.

Should the same be said of polls?

Writes Ladd, quoting population geneticist R. C. Lewontin of Harvard University, "Sometimes we let our wishes shape our understanding of what is—even to the point of collecting data in a way which otherwise would be seen as flawed." So, taking D'Antonio's Virginia example, it seems likely that Lewontin is correct. Major Republican donors in Virginia have since banded together to pressure Virginia's conservative Republican governor George Allen to improve Virginia's deteriorating education, or else.

Surveys can be screwy. Polls do show—as Gingrich said—that people want smaller government, that they want many federal programs shifted to the state (presumably for better oversight and to reduce costs), but that they still want the government. They don't want programs that affect them tampered with. They want government there for their own and their parents' Social Security and health care, and for a variety of other programs. Their motivations are not just selfish: 66 percent of men and 72 percent of women, for example, want government to fund job training.

Polls ask people yes-or-no questions when reality is not

that way; people might say they're against welfare if that's the question that's asked, but what might emerge with more detailed questions is that they are against the system as it stands because they think many welfare recipients get more money than they need. Or, poll respondents may be against Home Assistance but for AFDC. So, in fact, people who are asked, "welfare: yes or no?" may answer no even while they're part of a majority who think there's some place for government assistance.

Detailed polls, by contrast, show that the majority of Americans have a highly nuanced approach to welfare. A 1994 CBS-*New York Times* poll and a 1995 NORC poll showed in concert that while 58 percent of the people CBS-NYT polled believed welfare recipients were "getting more than they need," 57 percent of the respondents (NORC) still wanted to assist the poor. Were they the same people? Pollsters would say yes.

Polls will tell you that conservative voters and their religious allies elected a Republican Congress in order to halt abortion; certainly many politicians welcomed the support. But in Washington, pro-life versus pro-choice is a political question before it's a moral one. Republican congresswomen told their leaders that sticking antiabortion measures and provisions on legislation would cost Republicans at the ballot box. And so by August 1995 the pro-life forces could only watch as the House of Representatives voted to fund family planning.

The Christian right is anti-abortion. Candidate Pat Buchanan, for example, warned that if the Republicans abandon the fight against it, there will be a third party. The overwhelming majority of Christian Coalition members oppose abortion. However, the Christian Coalition's Ralph Reed (who supported Gingrich's Contract with America by spending $1 million of the coalition's money on informational mailings) must balance Congressional reality with the coalition's desire to see its own ten-point Contract with the American Family transformed into legislation.

What do the polls say about the Christian right? Princeton University sociologist Robert Wuthnow interprets the opinion surveys this way: "I don't sense that the Christian Coalition has the clout to blackmail the Republican Party into doing anything. If you look at polls over the last twenty years, since the Moral Majority got started in the late seventies, there isn't any stronger support now than then for fundamentalism or some of these very conservative Christian orientations."

Recent Gallup survey figures, he said, show that the Christian Coalition and the religious right are "pretty small. Maybe 10 to 12 percent of the adult population would feel some sympathy for it directly."

What the Christian Coalition did to arrive at its Contract with the American Family categories, said Wuthnow, was to very cleverly examine the polls to see where there was majority support for various issues. He points out that virtually everything in that contract "is, on an issue-by-issue basis, supported by a majority of people in at least some polls." But polls are politics; in the real world, issues do not come so neatly separated and individuals still defy easy categorization.

One issue the majority of Americans said they favored was "returning education control to the local level" by abolishing the Department of Education.

Though the majority of Americans probably do not know what the Department of Education does, the idea of abolishing any federal department to increase local funds and local control has a sensible ring to it.

Similarly, most Americans favor some sort of prayer in public places, including schools, though most may not have thought through the specifics. Knowing this sympathy toward the idea, as revealed in polls, the Christian

Coalition's lead-off item in its Contract with the Family is "Restoring Religious Equality: a constitutional amendment to protect religious liberties of Americans in public places."

The Congressional Republican majority, keeping faith with a Christian Coalition that had supported its candidacies, held hearings around the country to gauge the popularity of this alternative to the separation of Church and State. The amendment's critics contend this would lead to mandated school prayers, and would force a particular religious entity's—the Religious Right's—interpretation of Christianity down the throats of believers and nonbelievers alike.

If nothing else, the contentious hearings revealed that Americans had not been polled in sufficient detail—many might like the idea of school prayers, but they also favor the separation of Church and State as a safeguard to religious minorities.

The amendment's proposals, which would allow or mandate school prayers, created a new cohesion among Jewish, mainline Christian groups, and the traditional "peace" churches (such as Quakers and Mennonites) showing strong opposition to tampering with the current Constitutional guarantees, despite the polls. This cohesion may not directly affect the 1996 presidential election, but it does reflect the tendency in American history that as one extreme of the political spectrum gains strength, Americans gradually unite to create a countervailing force.

How *does* all this translate into 1996 election results? One White House adviser, once again trying to interpret the polls, noted, "Polls show that only five percent of the people knew anything about the Contract with America. What voters really wanted to do was kick the Democrats out," he said—ruefully, one assumes, because he was one of the strategists for the 1994 Democratic Congressional elections that ended in a rout. "They wanted to kick out people they felt were stopping the political system, the governmental system, from working properly. I think, from the latest polls, that people do sense that things are happening for the better, that there is change. If so, all the incumbents are going to benefit. The President will benefit, the Republican Congress will benefit."

What is the alternative to polling? Reading entrails? Gut instinct? Anyone who has been on the campaign trails with this year's crop of presidential candidates and has actually listened to, or interviewed, Americans turning out to hear the candidates, comes away reassured that the American electorate is actually less knee-jerk, more thoughtful, than the Congressional Republicans of the right might desire.

Whatever encouragement might be coming from talk radio and snap polls, mature Americans (and the polls say the last crop of voters were the educated and better-off), who buy Republican candidates' fund-raising dinner tickets, in conversation are by no means all knee-jerk rightwingers, or one-issue conservatives.

Over coffee, beer, wine, or Perrier or scotch, many of those putting up big bucks to listen to the candidates, as they relax into a conversation on the subtleties of the issues, sound a lot more like Rockefeller Republicans than Reagan Republicans. The nation's biggest national poll— the election day vote—will decide whether that observation is correct or not.

Issues, like politicking, require compromise, and compromise does not easily show up in the infinitely less complex, for-or-against, yes-or-no attitudes that polls measure. So, for example, on the Gingrich Contract with America, while polls may show voters approve of the Republicans' initial steps, the actual cuts, which will affect people in ways they haven't yet imagined and which necessarily will be implemented through a messy process of politicking, may not be what people had in mind when they signaled their approval to the pollsters.

Therefore, the point is again, that the polls may not reflect voters' attitudes sufficiently *in their entirety*.

So what happens when you put polls and people together? Try the supermarket aisle for answers. The Food Marketing Institute's 1995 survey shows that crime, including youth crime and people carrying guns, worries Americans most. The Christian Coalition has got its finger on the broad brush issues, even if its proposed solutions may not be so broadly acceptable. The FMI poll showed that the breakdown of the family unit, accompanied by a lack of morals, religious faith, values, and work ethic, is Americans' second-greatest anxiety.

What are this year's candidates to make of another aspect of the FMI poll—the one that shows that three out of four Americans are more likely to remain loyal to their primary supermarkets than they are to their political party?

More, 52 percent of all Democrats and 48 percent of all Republicans, according to a spring 1995 poll, favor the formation of a third political party. But does that mean those same people would actually vote for those third-party candidates?

The polls didn't ask.

SPEAKING TO THE SILENT MAJORITY

NAME: Patrick Joseph Buchanan
BORN: November 2, 1938
EDUCATION: B.A., Georgetown University; M.A., Columbia
      University
OCCUPATION: Television commentator
FAMILY: Married to Shelley Buchanan
QUOTE: "I believe the other Republicans in the field . . .
      are leap-year conservatives."

PAT BUCHANAN HAS GONE FROM AGGRESSIVE ACTIVISM
to being a controversial television commentator and a pri-
mary-spoiler, all without ever having been elected to any
public office. Now he wants to be President, and men who
have spent a lifetime in politics and are the leading contenders for the Republican Party nomination are having
nightmares about New Hampshire crowds that chant, "Go,
Pat, go!"

Buchanan's candidacy proves that you do not have to
be elected to anything to be a winner in politics. He
proved that in 1992, when he went from who's-he-kidding
status to giving George Bush the scare of his life in New
Hampshire. In fact, Buchanan's showing in that primary,

with 37 percent of the vote, was so strong that he was
rewarded with a speaking slot at the Republican National
Convention. There he probably fatally wounded any
chances Bush had for reelection with a speech attacking
abortion rights, homosexuality, immigration, NAFTA,
current moral standards, and a whole range of liberal
touchstones, delivered with a zeal that appalled most of
his listeners but won raves from the far right of the GOP.
As for what happened to Bush, Buchanan is unrepentant.

Now he is set to attack again. What has senior
Republican Party veterans and the leading candidates
trembling is the possibility that Buchanan may prove so
popular in the early primaries that he will control the GOP
platform and take it so far to the right on so many issues
that in comparison the Goldwater disaster of 1964 will
look like a vote of public confidence. It is Buchanan the
political player, not Buchanan the prospective President,
who has candidates such as Bob Dole and Phil Gramm
worried; while his chances of being elected are marginal,
he could wreck the prospects of most of the front-runners
just to make sure the party adheres to his conservative
agenda.

That charge is old news, Buchanan responds. He's
already won control of the GOP agenda. "When you have
Jack Kemp talking about shutting down HUD [the
Department of Housing and Urban Development], when
Dick Lugar talks about abolishing the IRS, when Pete
Wilson talks about illegal immigration and Bob Dole calls
for a cultural war for the soul of America, then it isn't the
George Bush Republican party anymore; it is the
Buchanan party."

The key to understanding Buchanan's view of his candidacy is his conviction that his heroes and mentors—
Richard Nixon and Ronald Reagan—were successful
when they stuck to their conservative instincts, against

advice to the contrary from their political strategists. When they temporized, Buchanan argues, Nixon and Reagan usually failed politically, too.

The fifty-six-year-old Buchanan comes to his political theory through personal experience and close observation. After college at Georgetown University and a master's degree in journalism from Columbia University, in 1966 the youthful Buchanan joined Nixon's campaign as a speechwriter. Once Nixon was elected President, Buchanan went to the White House, and he stayed on as a press advisor to Gerald Ford. He was Reagan's White House communications director from 1985 to 1987, and since then he has been a visible talking head on conservative issues through his syndicated newspaper column and shows on radio and television.

Where Buchanan's campaign rhetoric bites hardest is with his appeals to the dissatisfied center-right of American voters, people who have wandered through the American political wilderness, flirting with George Wallace, disdaining Jimmy Carter, rushing to Reagan, and taking a chance on Bill Clinton.

"Americans distrust their government. They think the whole country is being sold out to some kind of global new world order," Buchanan argues. "My strength is with the Reagan voters—Democrats, Catholics, ethnics—and the Perot voters. The social conservatives are much more dedicated to the politics of ideas, and they will walk. Liberals don't tend to walk; they tend to talk."

Buchanan dismisses the Clinton White House as "the children's hour." He reserves special scorn for his more immediate rivals, especially front-runners Dole and Gramm. He particularly bristles at the mention of the Texas senator, who many Republicans say might make a more credible conservative alternative to Dole.

Buchanan calls Gramm a "leap-year conservative" for

his votes to confirm Supreme Court justice Ruth Bader Ginsburg, to continue aid to the handicapped, and in favor of foreign aid. He says that Gramm and others "have bought into the myth of economic man, that everything can be solved with tax cuts, balance the budget, get the numbers right, [and then] the problem is solved. It's a myth, and everyone knows it."

He calls Dole an Eisenhower Republican in a Gingrich-Buchanan age. "His record is of supporting every single tax increase in the 1980s," Buchanan says, and points out that Dole supported the liberal 1991 trade quota bill, NAFTA, GATT, the World Trade Organization, and continued funding for the Agency for International Development.

But where Buchanan gets the crowd on its feet is when he talks about his "religious war for the cultural soul of America." His stump speech is a tirade against abortion and affirmative action and advocates America-first policies in defense, trade, and foreign aid. On immigration, he goes California's Proposition 187 movement one better: He would declare a five-year moratorium on legal immigration and build a fence along two hundred miles of the United States–Mexico border.

And when Buchanan has spoken, the otherwise silent majority within the GOP ranks has responded. In a straw poll among Virginia Republicans, Buchanan scored an upset win that left Dole and Gramm running a distant third and fourth, respectively. In Arizona, a state that has an early primary and which has usually been considered Phil Gramm's territory, Buchanan whipped Gramm again, getting 76 percent of straw-poll votes after the two of them spoke from the same platform. In New Hampshire he has run strongly enough to dissuade that state's popular governor, Steve Merrill, from endorsing Gramm. Merrill now tells anyone who will listen that his state will probably give Dole a win and Buchanan a second-place finish.

With a limited war chest (less than $2 million), Buchanan has to win big and early. To that end, Republican Party leaders are trying to shut off his flow of funds and snuff out his campaign as soon as possible. Would-be contributors have been discouraged from giving to Buchanan, and possible allies—including the Christian Coalition's Ralph Reed—have been coaxed into wondering whether Buchanan can indeed win.

Buchanan himself is unfazed. Particularly when it comes to the right-to-life plank that he wedged into the GOP platform three years ago, Buchanan refuses to negotiate. If he and it are rejected, he warns, he will start a third-party campaign of his own and plug on. It is that prospect that bothers the Dole wing of the party most of all.

PRIORITIES

1. Repeal NAFTA and end U.S. aid to Mexico
2. Crack down on Japanese trade protectionism
3. End most foreign aid, including contributions to the World Bank and to Israel
4. Cut federal support of Medicare and aid to veterans and farmers
5. End affirmative action
6. Enact strict anti-abortion laws
7. Institute tougher anti-crime measures

ALL THAT GLITTERS . . .

NAME: Malcolm Stevenson Forbes, Jr.
BORN: July 18, 1947
EDUCATION: B.A., Princeton University
OCCUPATION: Editor and publisher
FAMILY: Married to Sabina Forbes; five children
QUOTE: "We're going to have to go to a monetary system like Bretton Woods. Not fixed exchange rates, but anchored to something like that four-letter word: g-o-l-d."

IN HIS FAIRLY RARE TELEVISION APPEARANCES, Malcolm S. "Steve" Forbes, Jr., probably appears to the public as an earnest, almost diffident contrast to his late, high-profile father, he of the hot-air balloons and fabulous parties at his Tangier palace. While Steve is the third generation of Forbeses to head *Forbes* magazine, quick father-son comparisons risk missing some points. Both Malcolm and son Steve were ahead of the respective popular waves of their times.

When the next U.S. President takes office in January 1997, says Steve Forbes, the economy will look the same as today: slow. That annoys Forbes; given the economy's potential, given the fact that the Cold War is over, given the burgeoning high-tech revolution, "we should be growing at twice the rate we are today—at least 5 or 6 percent in real terms." Should anyone care what Forbes predicts? Well, yes, given (a) that he is making a presidential bid on which he'll spend $25 million of his own money, and (b) that he's also the only financial writer ever to have won the USX Crystal Owl award four times for the accuracy of his economic forecasting.

His economic opinions, by contrast, are already firmly set. To Steve Forbes, the deficit-cutting battle would be half won just through a flat tax and lowered interest rates. One of the top priorities of the new President, he says, must be to remove obstacles to the realization of the U.S. economy's full potential. Forbes contends that a smart step would be going back to a version of the gold standard. Fair economic weather or foul, he says, gold will bring low interest rates, with the average family getting a thirty-year fixed mortgage at under 5 percent interest.

Real savings from budget reform, he says, should be earmarked to increase personal exemptions for children so that people can see a direct connection between reducing the budget and taking pressure off families raising children.

Steve is more conservative personally and politically than his father, who was both a moderate Republican and a modern-day Barnum. As a student at Princeton, he founded a magazine called *Nation's Business* (still going strong a quarter-century later), and at *Forbes* Steve pursued a more right-wing course, not just in his editorials but by bringing on board as Forbes columnists such conservatives as Michael Novak of the American Enterprise Institute and Hoover Institution economist Thomas Sowell.

Steve, like his father, has been a player in New Jersey politics—as an early backer and advisor to Governor Christine Todd Whitman. As *Forbes* editor-in-chief since Malcolm's death in 1990, Steve Forbes has made his "Fact and Comment" columns a rallying point for business and political conservatives. He is chairman of the board of Empower America, a think tank based in Washington, D.C.; Newt Gingrich is also on the organization's board, and William J. Bennett and Jack Kemp are co-directors.

Like them, Forbes has both a chopping list and a shopping list. For the chop: the departments of Commerce, Housing and Urban Development, Energy, and Education, and government assistance or direction to defense contractors as the industry consolidates. He'd shop around for a NAFTA-like agreement first with Japan and then eventually with other Pacific Rim countries, and for a new defense strategy while moving ahead with a mobile strike force and eventually a full-scale Star Wars anti-missile system. His health-care prescription would introduce medical savings accounts, and he would give grants to people over 65: "Give them $2,000. Let them be liable for the next $2,000," he says, "then cover everything above that."

Though Forbes is still close to the Republican party, he believes a third-party candidate can make it. "People are not happy with the politics of the present," he says, "and that's why we got that turnaround in November 1994 and why they're not very happy with the current crop of announced candidates." Looking at the electorate, Forbes does not classify Perot voters as a group but as people who "are very unhappy with the system and leadership they're getting."

Though he will make every effort to win, there is one man—not yet announced as a candidate, as of this writing—to whom Forbes would defer: Newt Gingrich. In the case of such a candidacy, said Forbes during an interview, he would weigh in where he would be most effective, "pushing issues, like Larry Kotlow and I did with Christine Whitman."

How does he regard his candidacy? "As the kids would say," he replied, "awesome."

PRIORITIES

1. Anchor the dollar to a gold standard
2. Reform Social Security
3. Reform or eliminate the Federal Reserve system
4. Institute a 17 percent flat tax
5. Push pro-growth supply side economics

AMERICA'S FIRST JEWISH PRESIDENT?

NAME: Arlen Specter
BORN: February 12, 1930
EDUCATION: B.A., University of Pennsylvania; LL.B.,
      Yale University
OCCUPATION: United States senator
FAMILY: Married to Joan Levy Specter (a Philadelphia city
      council member); two children
QUOTE: "I will lead the fight to strip the strident anti-
      choice language from the Republican national
      platform and replace it with language that respects
      human life—but also respects the diversity of
      opinion within our own party on this issue."

SENATOR ARLEN SPECTER HAS THE UNIQUE DISTINC-
tion among the announced Republican candidates for
President of having an endorsement from another Republican candidate for President: publisher Malcolm S.
Forbes, Jr.

Back in March 1995, Forbes saluted Specter as "the
most outspoken pro-choice GOP White House aspirant"
and argued that he "has a chance to leap into the first tier
now that he has proposed a variant of House majority
leader Dick Armey's flat-tax proposal." To get ahead of
Specter, Forbes advised, rivals Bob Dole, Phil Gramm, and

Lamar Alexander had better come up with flat-tax plans of their own or be left in Specter's wake.

Since then, Specter's leap into the front ranks has fallen considerably short. And as for the front-runners, their enthusiasm for a flat tax has been perfunctory at best; after all, the credit would only go to Representatives Armey and Gingrich.

But the senior senator from Pennsylvania is not dismayed. He continues a unique struggle for the Republican Party's soul in 1996. While candidates Bob Dole and Phil Gramm are pulled ever further to the right in the backwash of Pat Buchanan's jeremiads, Specter is firmly entrenched left of center—a throwback to an era when the GOP tent covered moderate-to-liberal individuals such as Jacob Javits, Nelson Rockefeller, and William Scranton.

Arlen Specter truly defines himself by how he differs from the Gingrich-Gramm-Armey wing of the party. He is from a northern state, Jewish, pro-choice on abortion, and critical of the Christian Coalition and of talk about a "holy war" for American culture. He doesn't even like the Contract with America.

With splendid effrontery, Specter has unveiled his own Commitments to America, a ten-point platform that calls both for balancing the budget through spending cuts and for using the savings to reduce the national debt. As noted, he is for a flat tax. Specter is tough on crime, would crack down on repeat offenders, and would make greater use of the death penalty. He opposes gun control. He believes in the privatization of education and private-public funding of "charter schools," which will stress the latest in high-technology teaching; on health care, he believes in the free-market approach; on international affairs, he would follow an activist foreign policy and focus on attacking terrorism around the world as a key to his defense strategy. And, yes, he is resolutely pro-choice.

If the women of America are aware of Specter's position on the abortion debate, they have not rushed forward in gratitude. Specter still suffers from the rage many feminist leaders rained down on him for his sharp questioning of Anita Hill when she accused Supreme Court nominee Clarence Thomas of making sexual advances. Despite being one of the more ardent pro-women voices in the Senate, Specter was written out of the movement and narrowly won reelection in 1992 against a female opponent. All his pro-choice stance has produced is scorn from the Christian right.

Specter could care less. "Let me say it as plainly as I can: Neither this nation nor this party can afford a Republican candidate so captive to the demands of the intolerant right that we end up reelecting a President of the incompetent left."

Specter reserves special scorn for his former comrade in the pro-choice ranks, California Governor Pete Wilson, whose early campaign self-destructed. Wilson's increasingly lukewarm stance on the abortion issue, plus his backing of other right-wing notions such as a crackdown on immigration, all helped Specter's candidacy, the senator believes.

Specter must win big in the early caucuses and primaries if he is to survive. Can Specter make it? Some say yes. In the Iowa caucus, all the GOP hopefuls will be hoping to take a big enough chunk out of front-runner Bob Dole's lead there to springboard them into New Hampshire and toward greater glory. Counting Robert Dornan, Alan Keyes, and the five better-known candidates, that makes seven right-leaning conservatives jousting for the support of that wing of the Iowa party. It leaves Specter alone in the center and with a strong appeal to GOP women.

Specter strategists figure that if their man can get just

17 percent of the vote in Iowa, he would win the state outright, since the other candidates would split the rest. Then if Specter could poll just about the same in New Hampshire—and there is a precedent, since Warren Rudman won in 1980 against four rivals with just 30 percent—he would be off and running.

But will he? At this point, it is doubtful. But again, Specter doesn't seem to care that he is alone in his quest, largely ignored by the media, derided by the leaders of his party, and basically unknown to the GOP activists who must turn out in the spring to make their choices. Specter is used to being alone, and tenacity is his defining trait.

Specter's Russian-Jewish immigrant parents moved him to Russell, Kansas—Bob Dole's hometown—when he was quite young. His isolation there led to an obsessive study of baseball statistics and a determination to get into public life. He got his wish, but his political career has had as many downs as ups. After a stint as a staff lawyer on the Warren Commission, Specter lost a bid to be mayor of Philadelphia. He won the city prosecutor's job for four terms, lost it, lost a race for the Senate in 1976, and failed to be elected governor in 1978. He won his Senate seat in 1980 and has survived two challenges.

"All that means," Specter said in an interview, "is that I am seven and four in eleven races. I have had more tough campaigns than any of my opponents, so I am not here to fall in line. I'm the only guy who can beat Pat Buchanan, Ralph Reed, and Pat Robertson. I even opposed Oliver North. In 1996 I intend to win the White House."

Perhaps if he picks Steve Forbes as his vice president . . .

PRIORITIES

1. Remove the anti-abortion plank from the Republican Party platform

2. Implement a flat tax to replace current federal income tax
3. Impose a federal death penalty on convicted terrorists
4. Repeal NAFTA
5. Reform Medicare and welfare programs

Part Two

PLAYERS AND SPOILERS

THE CHRISTIAN COALITION
AND RALPH REED

IN SEPTEMBER 1995 SIX CANDIDATES FOR THE Republican presidential nomination—seven if Newt Gingrich runs—genuflected before a 4,000-strong Christian Coalition crowd over a two-day period in a bid to bring the religious right's organizational might to their campaigns. It was as compelling a demonstration as anyone could ask for to show how far the coalition had come from its founding by religious broadcaster Pat Robertson only six years earlier.

But in a sense, the Christian Coalition is after bigger game than the next occupant of the White House. It wants to dominate the Republican Party by controlling the state parties, Robertson told the delegates, who represented the coalition's 1.7 million members. That way the coalition would, in time, get the White House anyway.

Ralph Reed, Jr., the thirty-four-year-old executive director of the coalition, told the gathering, "Let me be clear, we did not come from every corner of this nation to endorse any candidate, annoint any front-runner, be courted or married to any prospective presidential nominee. The question as we head into 1996 is not who we endorse. The question is, 'who will endorse our agenda?'"

One answer may be Pat Buchanan. Though the coalition did not say so, in a gesture that endorsed him more directly, the program yielded to Buchanan founder Pat Roberson's customary spot as dinner keynote speaker.

The Christian Coalition is a carefully split-screen entity that shows one image to its members: an anti-abortion evangelical and fundamentalist Christian organization working from Scriptural injunctions and high nationalism; and yet another image to those it would impress, and serve, politically—that of the astute, doctrinally flexible on abortion, precinct-worker-wise operative.

The duality works, though the coalition rhetoric does include helping itself to a large share of other people's victories. Yet Reed could honestly remind the crowd, "Think back to just one year ago in this city, in this hotel, this very week, and what has transpired since you and I last gathered together: Tom Foley has been replaced by Newt Gingrich. George Mitchell has been replaced by Bob Dole. Howard Metzenbaum, one of our favorite members of the U.S. Senate, has been replaced by pro-life, pro-family Roman Catholic Mike DeWine."

The Christian Coalition is doing very well in this Congress, as was illustrated four months earlier, in May 1995, when the scene was the Mansfield Room on the Senate side of the U.S. Capitol. At center stage was Reed, later billed on *Time* magazine's cover as "The Right Hand of God." Not facing the media barrage, but still very much present, was Reed's boss, Robertson, himself a 1988 candidate for the presidency. Surrounded by the coalition's state chairmen, flanked by House Speaker Newt Gingrich and Texas senator and presidential candidate Phil Gramm, Reed was confronted by a dozen television cameras and forty print journalists. Reed was about to unveil his ten-point

Contract with the American Family as the coalition's add-on to Gingrich's Contract with America.

The coalition has supported Gingrich's contract, said Reed, in part because it dealt with economic issues such as a balanced federal budget, welfare reform, and a flat tax. The Christian Coalition supports balancing the budget not only because they believe it is fiscally well-advised but also because they oppose the notion that one generation would run up its debt and saddle it on the next generation. "That," said Reed—who is not an ordained minister; his doctorate is in history from Emory University—"is not only an economic principle, it's a moral principle, in our view."

The coalition supports a tax-cut package that would allow families to receive a $500-per-child tax credit for every child in a family with an income under $200,000 a year. Reed has argued that the average American family of four paid just 2 percent of their adjusted gross income in federal income taxes in 1950, whereas in the 1990s that figure is 24 percent, or 39 percent if state and local taxes and value added tax (VAT) are included. Reed says that eliminating this crushing economic burden on the family is one of the coalition's top legislative priorities.

Reed, who says he was born again while musing and schmoozing in a Washington bar a decade ago, had worked on Gingrich's campaigns and was a leader of student Republicans while in college but decided to cast around for something deeper. He teamed up with Pat Robertson to create the Christian Coalition, the successor to the Reverend Jerry Falwell's Moral Majority, which went out of business shortly after Robertson's failed presidential bid.

Reed sees some overlap between the Christian Coalition and Ross Perot's United We Stand America (UWSA). "[Perot's supporters] tend not to be as worked up about issues like prayer and abortion," he suggested, "but on 80 percent of what we work on behalf of, they agree. And on about 90 percent of what they work on behalf of, we agree. So there's real overlap. Both [UWSA and the Christian Coalition] are grassroots in location, populist in style, outsider in orientation, [and] interested in really transforming American politics from the outside in."

In his own setting, Reed is a man of some charisma. Reed looks sort of like a religious, right-wing, darker-haired version of the character played by Michael J. Fox in the film *Doc Hollywood*—the type who can still lean heavily on his image of boyish winningness in public displays. This masks a behind-the-scenes toughness.

Reed is not Robertson's only channel to the religious right's masses, however. There is also the Christian Broadcasting Network (CBN), which Robertson built up from a defunct Portsmouth, Virginia, television station in 1967. CBN's mission statement is "to prepare the United States of America, the nations of the Middle East, Far East, South America, and other nations of the world for the coming of Jesus Christ and the establishment of the Kingdom of God on earth. We are achieving this end through the strategic use of mass communications, especially radio, television, and film, the distribution of cassettes, films, and literature, and the educational training of students to relate biblical principles to those spheres of human endeavor to play a dominant role in our world."

The 700 Club, CBN's twenty-year-old daily television newsmagazine, reaches a million households, and Robertson's on-screen fund-raising ability is phenomenal. When Robertson made his presidential bid in 1987–88 and resigned as an ordained minister to do so, he also absented himself from the CBN fund-raising scene. The ministry's income reportedly dropped by a third in twelve months, from $130 million to $83.5 million.

Subsequently Robertson formed International Family Entertainment (IFE) to buy the Family Channel from CBN for $250 million. Two years after that, in 1992, Robertson took IFE/Family Channel public. According to the *Congressional Record,* Democratic congressman Fourtney "Pete" Stark of California said, "The Robertsons put up $150,000—2.2 cents a share—and a minority shareholder put up $22 million. . . . IFE/Family Channel went public at $15 a share and [the Robertson family retains] 69 percent control." Plus CBN gained free air time for its *700 Club,* more or less in perpetuity, from what is the nation's seventh-largest cable television company.

According to published reports, Robertson said the sale made more than $600 million for CBN and $90 million for his family, most of which he gave to CBN.

"The bottom line," said CBN's vice president for public affairs, Gene Kapp, "is that the main beneficiary was CBN." Today Pat Robertson's businesses also own the Ice Capades; Standard News, a news service based in Washington, D.C.; an airplane charter company; a travel agency; and a hotel and convention center in Virginia Beach.

While Robertson has sold some of his IFE stock, he maintains a major stake in the company, which is the only operation from which Robertson draws a salary—$281,000 in 1993 with a $152,000 bonus. And while he has shelved his own political career, Robertson now has a proxy in Reed.

The Robertson/Reed duo has what *Wall Street Journal* columnist Albert R. Hunt calls a "good cop/bad cop routine." Hunt writes of "the calculated politics practiced by the resourceful Mr. Reed and his eccentric boss, the Reverend Pat Robertson . . . where the powerful Robertson/Reed empire seeks respectability in the corridors of Republican power, but also protects its flanks by feeding its flock the red meat of divisive issues."

Not divisive in Republican corridors is the idea of welfare reform. Reed said in an interview that "welfare reform for us isn't just about saving money. We have got to reduce the overwhelming amount of government subsidies to out-of-wedlock births. We believe it is skyrocketing illegitimacy, not only in the inner cities but frankly in the suburbs and the white community as well as in the black community. It's tearing apart the social fabric of America. It's about strengthening families. It's about restoring values."

What does Reed believe Christians should do for the poor? He points to the Christian Coalition's Contract with the American Family, which includes a bill that would increase the amount of charitable giving by providing people with a tax credit, thereby enabling them to direct a certain portion of their income to a charity of their choice rather than to the welfare state.

Reed relies on Rand Corporation studies showing that only about thirty to fifty cents of every tax dollar dedicated to the poor actually gets into their hands; the rest of it is spent on bureaucracy and overhead. He contends that what he calls "faith-based charities" are more efficient, delivering a far greater percentage of every dollar to the poor. "There's no question about the fact that simply by restricting government subsidies for out-of-wedlock births you do not solve the ultimate problem—which is a need for stronger marriages, for strengthening the families, for restoring of values, for spiritual renewal, and for meeting the physical needs of the poor and the downcast," he says.

The coalition supports the general idea of a simplified flat tax but withholds judgment on any particular version until they can see how it affects middle-class families with children, which are their core constituency.

The Christian Coalition's economic contract does not include foreign aid, except where the security of Israel is concerned. On defense, however, the coalition takes a stand against the participation by American troops in NATO and UN operations. "We believe that Americans should only be commanded by their American commanders," Reed says.

What, precisely, is the Christian Coalition? A church? A quasi political party? Reed says that the coalition has "never claimed to be a church, we've never claimed to be a ministry, we've never claimed to speak for every person of faith or to speak with a pastoral voice.

"We are lay persons," he says, "citizens of faith who are speaking only for ourselves, not claiming to speak for God [but] concerned about the direction of our country. We do not endorse candidates. We do not recruit candidates. We do not contribute to candidates. We are an issues organization. So we are really sort of halfway in between: not a church, not a party, not a political organization, but also not a spiritual organization. We work on behalf of lower taxes on the family [and] tougher laws against crime and drugs. We're protecting innocent human life, and we're willing to work with any candidate or any officeholder of either party or of all parties in order to advance that objective."

Reed would not speculate on whether a Republican presidential candidate could win if the coalition did not endorse him. Reed also does not believe he would accept a Republican White House position if it was offered, and he isn't looking for political office himself—it seems.

"I don't think so," he said. But the political bug is an insidious virus. Reed added, "I think that I have found that you never rule something like that out, but it's again best not to speculate on it because it's just not consistent with what my plans are for my own future."

Sounds a little like Perot . . .

Beyond Robertson's and Reed's personalities, the

coalition's political power boils down to two active and
one passive threat to Republican candidates.

Though Reed washes his hands of endorsing candidates,
the coalition's "voter guides" are a crafty and thinly disguised substitute. Next, the coalition members can and do
get out the vote.

The passive threat is that if the Republicans do not come
up with a presidential candidate who measures up to coalition standards, those 1.7 million members can just sit on
their hands.

And if the candidate is pro-choice on abortion, or soft on
coalition issues, they probably will.

HIGH PRIEST ON THE HILL

NAME: Newton Leroy Gingrich
BORN: June 17, 1943
EDUCATION: B.A., Emory University; M.A. and Ph.D., Tulane University
OCCUPATION: Speaker of the U.S. House of Representatives
FAMILY: Married to Marianne Gingrich (second marriage); three children
QUOTE: "This is a crusade for the soul of America."

THERE IS NO SHORTAGE OF POLITICIANS WHO WANT TO be President but who lack the fiber to come in off the sidelines and get knocked around in the scrimmage. And who can blame them? As we have noted elsewhere, the 1996 campaign is not for the fainthearted.

It's worse when you have something big to lose if you don't win even your party's nomination. All that will happen to Pat Buchanan if his political star is extinguished is that he will have to go back to being a television commentator. But what if you are the most powerful Speaker of the House since Sam Rayburn?

It is a bittersweet world for Congressman Newt Gingrich, Republican of Georgia. Of all the candidates in the wings sweating out the filing deadlines for the spring primaries (most occur around Christmas), the Speaker is on

the sharpest of tenterhooks since he has almost more to
lose by running for President than he does if he passes on
the chance. But in order for him to have a clear opening to
get into the game, the impossible must happen: Nearly all
of the front-runners have to self-destruct very early in the
contest. Indeed, in Gingrich's case, Bob Dole has to stumble badly well before the filing deadlines for the primaries
if the Speaker is to inherit a place.

Gingrich can claim to lead the vanguard of the new
Republican revolution. And he can raise huge sums of
money through the GOPAC political action committee,
which he has chaired since 1986. A select list of more than
1,800 of the group's regular donors made it possible for
Gingrich to dispense $424,000 to other Republican candi-
dates during the 1994 election campaign and to raise
another $487,500 in the first three months of 1995.

And, of course, there was the Contract with America, a
Gingrich-backed manifesto adopted by the GOP
Congressmen as 1994's campaign platform and 1995's
reelection springboard. Post-election polls showed that voters were mostly unaware of just what the contract
promised at the time they voted. But the adoption by
Congress of most of the contract's major planks, such as a
tough budget deficit cutback, loosening key federal regulatory restraints on environmental and financial rules, tough
new anti-crime measures, and a rollback of many of the
perquisites that lawmakers and their staffs enjoy, has
played well in the press as the Gingrich machine has rolled
over Democrats and pushed the Senate Republican establishment into uneasy acquiescence.

What does Gingrich want? In his much-publicized book
To Renew America, he argues that "the key problems we
face are civilizational problems, they're not political problems. I argue that the whole collapse of the family, the
collapse of the inner city, the collapse of the school

systems, the emergence of the drug culture, the rise of violent crime, the whole range of things, are a function of a crisis in our civilization. They are not a function of the breakdown of bureaucracy, and we've been running around trying to deal with symptoms because there was no space in the public square to talk directly and candidly about our civilization."

It helps to remember that Gingrich is a college professor at heart; his ideas are first of all a distillation of other people's notions, plus his own bias toward volunteerism and a faith that the Founding Fathers constructed a model of society that is still valid today. In his argument he impresses the listener with a bewildering reading list of citations: Peter Drucker's teachings, the biography of General Motors organizer Alfred Sloan, the organizational genius of General George Marshall, and the talismanic writings of Alexis de Tocqueville and the Federalist Papers.

"We have had a thirty-year detour in American civilization as we tried to use the Great Society and the counterculture and multiculturalism and all the various ideas that the left thought might work. My message is that the left's world view is doomed to fail because it is out of touch with how people function. The genius of the Founding Fathers was that they started from human beings and worked back to models. Their goal was to avoid dictatorship," he said.

A Gingrich presidency would be marked, according to the Speaker's own admission, by a willingness to make daring experiments to revive our education system through market-oriented reforms ("I'd keep firing teachers until we got it right"), through massive rollbacks in intrusive federal regulations on business, an end to affirmative action, and a tough but flexible trade policy.

But can Gingrich ever be President? Probably not, he concedes, unless lightning strikes and the party vaults him to the front of the line. "My ideas play well, but I guess I'm just what the media experts call too hot an image," he confesses. Recent polls confirm that. Voters generally give Gingrich's performance high marks for leadership, but by a two to one margin they have an unfavorable image of the man himself.

For the moment, that leaves the Speaker in an enviable position. He leads the intellectual revolution of his party and of the House. If Dole is elected President, he could end up as boss of the entire Congress. To give all that up to run for President might be more of a risk than he cares to take.

PRIORITIES

1. Implement the GOP Contract with America
2. Pass a balanced-budget amendment to the Constitution
3. Enact tax cuts for the middle class
4. Cut spending on Medicare, Medicaid, and welfare programs
5. Pass tougher anti-crime measures and institute capital punishment
6. Expand block grants to local schools for education experiments targeted to disadvantaged children
7. End affirmative-action programs

KEEPING THE NEW DEAL
FLAME ALIVE

NAME: Richard Andrew Gephardt
BORN: January 31, 1944
EDUCATION: B.S., Northwestern University; J.D., University of Michigan
OCCUPATION: Minority leader of the U.S. House of Representatives
FAMILY: Married to Jane Anne Gephardt; three children
QUOTE: "I have said over and over again that President Clinton deserves reelection, and I support him in that effort."

LIKE HOUSE SPEAKER NEWT GINGRICH, RICHARD Gephardt, the minority leader in the House of Representatives, has more to lose by running for President than by not running. And in order for him to have his chance, the incumbent President would have to announce that he was not going to seek reelection—not a happy prospect at the best of times.

But Gingrich and Gephardt find themselves in vastly different positions within their own parties, even though each nominally heads his respective organization within the House. Gingrich is the torch bearer for the new revolutionaries on the Hill. Gephardt, on the other hand, is a vestigial candidate. As such, his position would be even more vexing if he actually takes the presidential plunge in 1996.

"Dick Gephardt clearly is doing things which would make a candidacy possible if and when events drove him toward it," says Democratic advisor Ted Van Dyck, who thinks it is a good idea.

The scenario is that the gathering clouds of Whitewater will finally force Bill Clinton to announce he will not seek reelection in order to preserve his party's chances of keeping the White House. In the scramble to pick up the fallen banner, party celebrities from Vice President Al Gore to Senators Sam Nunn of Georgia and Bill Bradley of New Jersey would find their way blocked by the advance planning of the fifty-four-year-old Gephardt, who has firmly locked on to the liberal Democratic image as well the potent hot-button issue of foreign trade.

Gephardt's liberal protectionist stance was honed during his failed race for the nomination in 1988. He was against NAFTA then and remains so today. But since the ratification of the treaty and the creation of the World Trade Organization earlier this year, Gephardt has added other strings to his bow—most notably a tax proposal that has a few progressive income tax levels in it (to appeal to liberals) yet is still basically flat enough to be acceptable to anti-tax conservatives.

As minority leader of the Democratic opposition inside the House, Gephardt has welded together a loyal following among his besieged party fellows and has set himself up as sort of a government-in-exile apart from the Clinton White House. He preempted Clinton's State of the Union speech with an impromptu press conference earlier in the evening. He has publicly criticized the White House's budget-balancing bill and the general failure of the President and his lobbyists to coordinate their opposition to the Gingrich Contract with America through him.

His appeal is to the old coalition of minorities, unions, and the working class that has kept the Democrats in power for more than sixty years. His strongest financial and political support comes from the AFL-CIO, and he is not about to abandon them now.

"For Democrats, the single, simple, fundamental task of our party in this Congress, in this decade, in this generation, is to fight for the standard of living of working families and the middle class. Everything else is secondary," he says.

Meanwhile he waits for lightning to strike.

PRIORITIES

1. Cut the top income tax rate for three out of four Americans to 10 percent
2. Increase taxes on fringe benefits, including pensions
3. Repeal NAFTA
4. Expand health-insurance coverage to all working families
5. Strengthen affirmative action
6. Pass tougher environmental laws

A B-2 AT THE INDY 500

NAME: Robert Kenneth Dornan
BORN: April 3, 1933
EDUCATION: Loyola Marymount University, 1950–53
OCCUPATION: Congressman
FAMILY: Married to Sallie Hansen; five children
QUOTE: "Last month I flew the B–2. Brought it in, landed it twice. None of the other candidates can do that."

"I GREW UP IN BEVERLY HILLS IN A NONWEALTHY family around a lot of wealthy kids and wealthy families," said California Congressman Bob Dornan, sixty-two, one of Congress's most widely traveled adventurers, "and I'll tell you the families that don't invest their money in jobs, in job creation, in building things that create work for other people—those who instead lavished their money on their kids or put it into their own pleasures, eventually get caught up by drugs or booze or pills."

Dornan has lived as he speaks—full blast. The Jesuit-educated Dornan joined the Air Force as a pilot in the world's first supersonic fighter wing. His subsequent exploits and world travels as a pilot, as a war correspondent in Vietnam, as a broadcast journalist flying mercy flights into Biafra in the 1960s, and in national activities from civil-rights voter registration to Congress, paint a picture of a compulsive doer. Dornan, for example, created the POW-MIA bracelets worn by ten million Americans in the late 1960s and early 1970s and the Prisoner of Conscience bracelets for Soviet Jewish and Christian dissidents during that era.

This is how he sees the national political and economic scene: "Today, like during the 1980s, the Democrats are wrong about the impact of Republican economic policies and the Republican view that the American people should be able to keep more of their hard-earned income," said Dornan, who has a 100 percent Congressional voting rating from the American Conservative Union (ACU).

Four items from the Dornan presidential-bid platform: Pass a flat tax en route to a consumption-based tax, raise defense spending, sign a balanced budget amendment, and knock the capital gains down to 5 percent as a temporary measure before eliminating it entirely.

When a reporter asks a question about capital gains, Dornan doesn't just answer the question, he targets it. In fact, stand back; former fighter pilot that he is, he blasts it to smithereens in a rapid-fire burst that reveals his talk-show background. The topic's in his sights and the answer already started before the questioner has finished.

"How can we compete with Germany and Japan when they have no capital gains taxes?" asks Dornan, who has been in Congress since 1976. "You must never, ever punish with taxation your brightest men and women who create jobs. It's just unbelievable to punish people for formulating capital and investing in job creation." Dornan, a Reaganesque conservative on the rightmost reaches of the current GOP presidential-candidate spectrum, continues, "Short on answers, and failing to make good on Bill Clinton's promise to cut taxes for middle-class Americans, the Democrats continue to incite class warfare—even though

70 percent of those who will benefit from the GOP's capital gains tax cut will earn less than $50,000," he contends.

On the noneconomic front, Dornan points out that he co-sponsored a term-limits bill with Dan Quayle in 1977. He is against gun-control law and for transferring every aspect of welfare to the local level. As far as foreign policy is concerned, he sees foreign aid as a "huge football. Do we get all the way down to zero the way Pat Buchanan wants? Of course not—but total, unilateral foreign aid that has the word *charity* stamped all over it must have the American flag on everything." And, not surprisingly, the man whose Beltway moniker is "B–1 Bob" for his championing of defense spending has a lot to say on that topic. In short, the preference of this congressman, who serves on the House National Security Committee and the Permanent Select Committee on Intelligence, is for a navy-based strategy.

How can a longshot candidate like Dornan win the Republican nomination? He answers by describing the event as the Indy 500: "Gramm has peaked and probably hit the wall; Buchanan is pushing but in a car that can only last three hundred miles; Lamar Alexander has damaged his suspension and dropped back; Steve Forbes looks terrified—not an Indianapolis-quality car." Dole's out there in the running, and Dornan's there, too; in his own words, he's "steadily making the laps—but obviously I need the cars ahead of me to start pushing one another."

Even so, Dornan is realistic enough to add, "My problem is getting the Bob Dornan story out. But there is no doubt in my mind, as conceited as it sounds, that Bob Dornan is the best-rounded of all these candidates." And he keeps adding to the list of what he can do: In June he flew the B–2 bomber. "None of the other candidates can do that," he said. Maybe B–1 Bob will now become known as B–2 Bob.

PRIORITIES

1. Limit foreign command of U.S. troops
2. Balanced budget amendment
3. Institute a flat tax at 17 percent en route to a national consumption tax that would eliminate all income tax
4. Eliminate departments of Education, Commerce, Housing and Urban Development, and Energy
5. Sign a human life amendment to the Constitution

THE PENSIVE OPEN MAN

NAME: William Warren Bradley
BORN: July 28, 1943
EDUCATION: B.A., Princeton University
OCCUPATION: United States senator
FAMILY: Married to Ernestine Schlant; one daughter, one
stepdaughter
QUOTE: "I was the tallest French-horn player in the high
school marching band."

BILL BRADLEY'S ANNOUNCED RETIREMENT, AT AGE
fifty-two, from the Senate after his current term ends may
mean the end of a public life best characterized by two magazine articles. In 1965 Bradley, then a twenty-one-year-old
Princeton student, already a star basketball player, was pro-
filed in the *New Yorker*. Thirty years later, the *Economist*
editorially urged Bradley to run, "as an independent, not a
Democrat," for the presidency of the United States.

A three-term Democratic senator, Bradley hasn't said
what he'll do, but he hasn't ruled out a run at the White
House. Of course, a man who could turn down a half-million-
dollar offer in 1965 to play for the New York Knicks and
instead study politics, philosophy, and economics as a
Rhodes scholar at Oxford University doesn't necessarily
do the expected.

To his Knicks teammates, Bradley was always destined for high office. They initially called him "Dollar Bill," allegedly for his frugal living style despite his lucrative contract, and the media adopted the nickname. But later, according to Knicks teammate Dave DeBusschere, his fellow players took to calling him "Mr. President."

William Warren Bradley was born in Crystal City, Missouri, a small town on the Mississippi River thirty miles south of St. Louis. His father was president of the local bank. He became a basketball star early, and surprised the universities with big-name basketball teams by choosing not one of them but instead going to Princeton. His exposure to politics began in 1964, when he worked as an intern on Pennsylvania governor William Scranton's presidential campaign, but he put that interest aside temporarily while a player with the New York Knicks. He retired from basketball in 1977 and the following spring announced his candidacy for the U.S. Senate. He has been in the Senate since, though in 1988 he narrowly survived a challenge by Republican Christine Todd Whitman, now New Jersey's governor.

The senator serves on the Senate Finance Committee, the Energy and Natural Resources Committee, and the Special Committee on Aging. Widely known as the author of the bill that eventually became the Tax Reform Act of 1986, he based his tax reforms on the principle that people of equal incomes should pay equal taxes. Despite a widespread belief among observers that special interests would prevail, Bradley succeeded in sharply reducing tax rates for all Americans by eliminating most corporate and individual loopholes in the tax code. It required taxpayers to pay their fair share, gave tax relief to families, and ensured that six million low-income working people would pay no federal tax.

Bradley believes that the United States will not be able

to compete in the world economy in the next century without significant reductions in the federal debt and deficit. The first and most important step that can be taken on the road back to fiscal responsibility, he has contended, as have so many declared presidential aspirants, is to dramatically reduce unnecessary government spending.

Arguing that government spends too much taxpayer money, often for the wrong purposes, he has proposed two principles to guide all federal funding decisions: one, that the proposal must be in the general interest of and essential to public life; and two, taxpayer funding must be the most cost-effective way to finance the proposal.

In 1994 the bipartisan Concord Council ranked Bradley third among all Senate Democrats for his anti-spending votes. And in the 103rd Congress alone, he offered amendments to appropriations bills that would have saved nearly $600 million. Too, Bradley is the author of the enhanced line-item veto proposal, a measure that grants the president authority to remove wasteful spending from appropriations and tax bills

Two years ago, in 1994, Bradley called for a "national rebellion against crime and violence," contending there is no single, simple solution. He wrote legislation, adopted in the 1994 crime bill, to greatly expand community policing and put a thousand new police officers on the streets nationwide. He is an advocate of tough gun control, and he authored legislation that proposes national handgun ID cards, registration of private handgun transfer, increased dealer fees, and a limit on purchases.

Bradley, who as a young Princeton student was present the night in 1964 when the U.S. Senate voted approval of the Civil Rights Act, has regularly spoken out against racism. His criticism was particularly pointed during the Bush Administration. In July 1991 he called on Bush to explain his own stands on race, beginning with his opposition to the Civil Rights Act when he ran for the Senate in 1964.

To deal with America's social and political dilemmas, Bradley told a February 1995 National Press Club audience, "we need a three-legged, not a two-legged, stool. The government and market are not enough to make a civilization. There must also be a healthy, robust civic center. Yet today there are fewer and fewer forums where people actually listen to each other. Without this third leg, the stool cannot provide support for a vital America."

Bradley outlined four urgent needs in the United States. One, the American family must be strengthened. Two, "we need to create more quality civic space. Three, we need a more civic-minded media." Four, in order to revitalize the democratic process, the financing of elections has to be taken out of the hands of special interests. When pressed by that National Press Club audience about his own political future, Bradley answered that he was "ambiguously definitive or definitively ambiguous." (He was also asked about the baseball strike, and he replied, "I won't comment on any sport that has a ball that is so small.")

Bradley is not just written about. He is a writer. His highly readable *Life on the Run,* about his years in professional basketball, was published in 1976 to acclaim and reissued in May 1995. In 1982 he wrote *The Fair Tax,* which he claims helped popularize the ideas that became the Tax Reform Act of 1986.

In a new introduction to the 1995 edition of *Life on the Run,* Bradley said that many people ask him which is the greater thrill, being a senator or being a member of a championship basketball team. He writes that the two experiences cannot really be measured against each other, but that they do have a few things in common: "Each brings its own peculiar wear and tear to the body and mind," he wrote in the new introduction. "But in the U.S.

Senate, the pressure of work and the tension of making decisions never let up. The season is never over. And the sense of impermanence is the same."

Nonetheless, even as Bradley was writing that, he decided his Senate season was over and that his third term would be his last. He had probably also read his own polls in New Jersey regarding his slim chances of being reelected to a fourth term.

To use a basketball metaphor, Bradley is now an open man: He either makes a White House bid now or he does indeed retire from American politics.

PRIORITIES

1. Deficit reduction
2. Election finance reform
3. Tough gun control
4. Create "a robust civic center—more civic space"
5. Restore opportunities to the underclass with a mix of capitalist and governmental support

POLITICS *IS* ECONOMICS: THE VIEW FROM THE CORPORATE SUITE

POLITICS IS MONEY AND BUSINESS IS MONEY, YET POLItics and business do not always go together in the ways one might immediately suppose.

It is undoubtedly a matter of both preference and prudence that a great many business leaders are registered independents. Equally true, business executives do not vote as a bloc, but vote for candidates based on their individual preferences.

So, for example, American Business Conference chairman George N. Hatsopoulos, who is also founder, chairman, and president of Thermo Electron Corporation, a Boston company with over $1 billion in annual sales, could say in midsummer 1995, "I voted for President Clinton. Chances are I would not in '96—partly depending, of course, on who the Republican is."

It is equally true that the corporate world is not a homogeneous one in terms of its political demands or expectations. Legislation or economic policy that pleases a major U.S. multinational corporation may not benefit the midsized corporation with sales that range somewhere from

$50 million to $1 billion a year. As Hatsopoulos, former chairman of the Federal Reserve Bank of Boston, explained, "Very large corporations are shrinking a lot in terms of employment; midsized companies provide all the employment growth in this country. And we have different objectives. They are much more trying to conserve what they've got, and we're trying to build things for the future. We clash all over the place."

The Washington-based American Business Conference (ABC), which Hatsopoulos chairs, is fourteen years old. Its one hundred members control corporations with an aggregate total of 450,000 employees and revenues exceeding $42 billion. ABC favors deficit reduction, savings, and investment incentives, and has worked with Senators Domenici and Nunn on their flat-tax proposals.

To be an ABC member, an executive must head a company growing in revenues or net income at a rate exceeding twice that of the U.S. economy. Executive director John Endean said ABC's priorities include securities-litigation reform, regulatory reform, and improving the U.S. public school system.

All these issues are as political as they are economic. As presidential candidates make their claims for bolstering the economy, it makes sense to listen to what the business executives who create jobs and profits want and don't want. The comments of four corporate CEOs who are members of ABC provide insights into U.S. job creation, the big changes expected in government itself, and some apparent absurdities in environmental regulation.

On balance, the four CEOs suggest that though the economy is doing reasonably well, President Clinton had—and blew—his chance to make major changes across the economic spectrum.

They do like his efforts on trade, though. To Clark A. Johnson, chairman and CEO of Pier 1 Imports, Inc., a

Texas-based corporation dependent on imports, Clinton's open-trade policies contrast markedly with a growing isolationist and protectionist mood in the new Congress, especially among the freshmen Republicans.

Johnson explained in an interview that while he does not agree with all that Clinton has done, he believes the President's instincts on trade have been "awfully good." Johnson, as head of a retail chain that imports everything from bedding to wicker and which has $700 million in sales annually, declared that "many of the seventy-three new freshmen Republicans don't have an aggressive attitude toward trade, and some of them are saying, 'Oh, I'm basically a protectionist,' and listening to the siren calls of Pat Buchanan." Johnson argues that the protectionist Republicans were wrong and that trade is the United States' number-one economic issue. He also believes that the country is soon going to find itself in a period of slower economic growth. In order for the United States to maintain, let alone enhance, its citizens' current standard of living, the country has to be committed to exporting those American products that have significant advantages over the competition and "plug them into those parts of the world growing faster than we are"—China, for example.

Tradition has kept the U.S. domestic market more important than the export market for many people, Johnson contended, which means Americans have not properly understood that the United States is competing against world traders who have smaller domestic markets and thus are forced to sell internationally. Many Americans still believe their country is the center of the economic universe, but the United States in fact is inextricably tied into a global economy that has no economic center as such.

One aspect of U.S. trade that people point to with anxiety is the trade deficit. But Johnson points out that, together, autos imported from Japan and oil account for two-thirds of the $150 billion deficit. He contends that the oil-imports trade deficit is a form of energy policy: When imported oil is relatively cheap, U.S. policy is, effectively, to use up other countries' oil and save our own for a later date. Politically, therefore, Johnson is attuned to those candidates who show they truly understand the U.S. stake in foreign trade.

ABC member John Adler's take on the interplay between economics and politics focuses on three issues: big government, the budget deficit, and the regulatory environment.

On the latter, Adler, chairman and CEO of Adaptec, Inc., in California's Silicon Valley, said the federal Environmental Protection Agency, like its state counterparts, was created "to make things better. But when are we finished? Let me give you an absurd example." Adaptec is required under California law, he said, to measure toxicity in the rainwater running off the corporation's parking lots. So everyone is required to hire a consultant to measure the toxicity of water going down the drain. "We're going to be spending more and more money [on these things]. I find that kind of absurd."

From the next President, the Budapest-born Adler, who joined Adaptec (a computer equipment and microcircuitry firm, with more than $500 million in sales annually) in 1985 and was named chairman in 1990, wants but two things—"backbone and leadership" and no micro-managing of the economy, not by the White House and not by Congress.

"I'm not in favor of tinkering with cutting taxes at the moment," said Adler, who began his electronics career as an engineer with IBM before moving to Amdahl Corporation, "but I think the current tax code is crazy." He wants some kind of consumption-based tax—something like what Senators Nunn and Domenici are proposing.

On trade—Adaptec has its own highly successful Japanese subsidiary—Adler is lukewarm toward the Clinton administration's activities, Secretary of Commerce Ronald Brown, and the entire Department of Commerce. "Brown's done some things to help companies like Boeing get exports," said Adler, "but I don't think Silicon Valley gets much help from him, other than potentially browbeating the Japanese to increase their semiconductor purchases." Adaptec's Japanese marketing and sales organization works with Japanese electronics manufacturers on its own, without Commerce's help, and as a result has introduced to the Japanese market products developed in the United States.

On the subject of the budget deficit, Adler, a registered independent who describes himself as socially liberal and fiscally conservative, wants everything "put on the block, every three- or four-letter acronym in the book: EPA, HUD, you name it."

Like Adler, Dan Colussy, CEO of Annapolis-based UNC, Inc. (formerly United Nuclear Corporation), can become a little exercised about environmental regulations, too, but his greater concern is about the underlying economy.

He contends that the economy does not feel as though it is experiencing a strong recovery. "What we see here is constant pricing pressure—all your earnings are going to be dependent on constantly taking expenses out, getting more efficient. Now all that's good, but we haven't had a breather on this. All our customers, several thousand, are looking to squeeze every nickel out of pricing."

Politically speaking, Colussy wants the government to apply common sense to "the environmental issue equation," but he still favors an environmental cleanup. "UNC was United Nuclear Corporation, and naturally we have had a lot of cleanups to do—now virtually complete, but not 100 percent complete. We've had to spend some $60 million in the last eight years," said Colussy, "and it's been a lot of money for our company," which has $370 million annually in sales.

Some 40 percent of UNC's work is defense-related: military aviation equipment aftermarket support, pilot training, aircraft engine overhaul. UNC also is heavily export-oriented, though it doesn't appear so at first glance.

"The weak dollar is a plus to us," said Colussy, an engineer with a long career in U.S. airline operations, including a stint as president and CEO of Pan American World Airways. Though aircraft and engines come to UNC from around the world for overhaul and servicing, the income is like that from exports, and UNC's four overseas offices are kept busy.

Closer to home, when Colussy looks at political Washington, he likes what the Newt Gingrich Contract for America seeks, particularly litigation reform and the effort to reduce the size of government. He wants a consumption-based tax system that promotes saving.

Colussy, a registered independent, admits that in business he has had more success under Democratic presidents than under Republicans. He likes what Clinton has done in the international trade arena. The President, says Colussy, insisted "on a level playing field" for the United States.

With the presidential race accelerating, Massachusetts-based Hatsopoulos, who was educated at the Athens National Technical University and MIT, said he would not likely vote for another former governor; it is more likely that he would vote for a senator. That would give Hatsopoulos a choice among three candidates: Dole, Lugar, and Specter.

"Lugar's a good solid person," said Hatsopoulos. "Dole, in order to have a chance, I think, will have to declare that he's running only for one term because of his age." Then, Dole could "bite the bullet, and say he was going to do what's right for the country—some very unpleasant things."

What these CEOs want is a President capable of staying a tough course in a time of continued economic change—a President who does what's necessary when he knows what he's doing and has enough sense to stay out of the way when he doesn't.

STILL SOMEBODY

NAME: Jesse Louis Jackson

BORN: October 8, 1941

EDUCATION: B.S., North Carolina Agricultural and Technical State University; Chicago Seminary

OCCUPATION: Minister and civil-rights activist

FAMILY: Married to Jaquiline Brown Jackson; two daughters, three sons

QUOTE: "The [Democratic] party is not a religion for me. It's a vehicle."

YOU DO NOT HAVE TO BE ELECTED TO OFFICE TO BE A significant political figure. Getting your voice heard above the tumult is a good enough reason for being a candidate, even if you don't win. But such a candidacy is not lightly undertaken, for you will win no praise from the candidates who must succeed in order for their contest to be worthwhile. You will be seen (rightly) as a spoiler. The race will be expensive, wearing, and unpleasant; plus, as the political fixer in the movie *The Candidate* wrote on the matchbook cover he gave to Robert Redford, "You will lose."

Nevertheless, of the dozens of Americans who will put their names on the presidential ballot in at least some of the fifty states, the Reverend Jesse Jackson is one of the quixotic characters who are worth noting at least for what their candidacies say about the current indifference the voters are exhibiting toward the list of establishment candidates being served up to them for 1996.

Jackson, fifty-four, may run as a Democrat out of revenge because President Clinton ignored him in 1992 after he had swung his support to the Arkansas governor. Or he may run as an independent. No matter, for the Jackson campaign would seek to use his considerable influence among African Americans and ultraliberal whites to hold the Democratic Party to its traditional commitment to affirmative action and social welfare grants to minorities.

Of all the longshot candidates, Jackson is the one President Clinton fears most, inside the Democratic Party or out. In his first bid in 1988, Jackson scored 23 percent of the delegate count; four years later the Rainbow Coalition, his band of enthusiastic supporters, so scared the Clinton camp that promises of a Cabinet-level post were offered to garner his support. Once elected, Clinton declined to honor his promises and has pushed Jackson out of sight wherever possible, reportedly at the urging of the President's close friend and adviser, National Urban League chairman Vernon Jordan.

But Jackson's possible candidacy threatens more than the loss of a vital core constituency. The charismatic populist leader is a painful reminder of how far Mr. Clinton has drifted away from traditional Great Society liberalism, a drift that has carried him on past the "sensible" liberalism of the Democratic Leadership Council and onward to the right, to something that might be called Republicanism Lite.

At the emotion-packed 1995 convention of the National Association for the Advancement of Colored People (NAACP) in Minneapolis, Jackson drew loud laughter and applause when he noted that President Clinton had indeed made a major commitment to affirmative action. In a little-noted speech, Jackson said the President supported time-tables, quotas, goals, quantifiability, and accountability.

"The trouble is, the President was talking about Japan. All we want for [poor] America is what [establishment] America wants from Japan—a level playing field," he concluded.

Two factors could prevent Jackson from entering his name on the lists for the presidency a third time. He is under intense pressure from other black leaders not to harm the Democrats' already thinning chances of keeping the White House. Related to that is the steady right turn of the Republican rhetoric as the primaries approach, a shift that threatens the liberal African-American agenda with an even less sympathetic alternative to Bill Clinton.

"The best scenario would be for me not to have to run," Jackson has been quoted as saying.

PRIORITIES

1. Implement massive disarmament, with the savings to be spent to create new affirmative action jobs
2. Tilt U.S. foreign policy away from Israel and toward a closer alliance with Arab nations
3. Institute tougher environmental laws
4. Toughen trade laws, especially with Japan
5. Repeal NAFTA
6. Enact higher taxes for the wealthy and put an end to loopholes that favor the rich
7. Implement tax cuts for the poorest Americans
8. Strengthen health care, Medicare, and Medicaid, especially for senior citizens

THE FATHER OF
AFFIRMATIVE ACTION

NAME: Arthur Allen Fletcher
BORN: December 22, 1924
EDUCATION: B.A., Washburn University of Topeka
OCCUPATION: Activist
FAMILY: Married to Bernyce Hasson Fletcher; six children
QUOTE: "I've worked on affirmative action all my life and
I can't stand there and let it all go down the
drain."

WHILE JESSE JACKSON CONTINUES TO LABOR WITHIN
the Democratic Party for the time being, the 1996 campaign
may be remarkable in part for the number of candidates for
the Republican nomination who are of African-American
birth. Arthur Fletcher can claim the longest career as a GOP
loyalist, and he has never had any doubts that he was in the
right party.

With a campaign that operates out of his house in
Washington, D.C., Fletcher is seeking campaign funds in
five-dollar increments and emphasizing the Republican
Party's obligation to avoid the attacks on affirmative action
and women's rights that are the stock in trade of many of
the front-runners.

At the same NAACP convention that cheered Jesse Jackson, Fletcher received polite but disbelieving attention to his crusade to push the GOP back to the middle.

"My concern, more than anything else, is to see to it that the party doesn't completely end up abandoning the middle, where the majority of voters live, in pursuit of the nomination. There's not a ghost of a chance of [my rivals] being nominated . . . unless they engage in the race-baiting, gender-bashing tactics of the moment," Fletcher said.

Fletcher comes by his concern through a long history of government service. In the first year of the Nixon administration, Fletcher was the Department of Labor official who created what was called the Philadelphia Plan, the first effort by Washington to break color barriers in the skilled-trades unions. The plan said federal contractors (first in Philadelphia and then elsewhere) had to meet minority job targets set by the Labor Department. It was the first affirmative-action plan, and it was unabashedly based on quotas. What most people forget in the current outcry over the abuses of affirmative action was that the Philadelphia Plan worked because it had narrowly targeted objectives.

Another strength is that Fletcher is very well plugged in with the establishment Republican party. He seconded Bob Dole's nomination to be vice president at the 1976 GOP convention and served successive terms as a civil-rights commissioner for Presidents Ford, Reagan, and Bush. His campaign will be a not-too-gentle warning voice heard inside the Republican primary scrimmage.

Fletcher is by no means from a privileged background. This is what makes his adherence to the self-help theology of the GOP all the more convincing. A wounded combat veteran of World War II, a distinction he shares with Bob Dole, Fletcher won his college education by being a star football player at Washburn University (Bob Dole's alma mater as well), where he earned Little All-America honors as a rushing back. He was one of the first black players to crack the National Football League's color barrier, playing for the Los Angeles Rams and later the Baltimore Colts.

He won national recognition within Republican Party circles for his skill as a community organizer of black voters for GOP candidates. In 1969 President Nixon named him assistant secretary of labor, and he rose quickly to become that agency's top compliance officer. President Nixon also appointed him a member of the U.S. delegation to the United Nations in 1971.

PRIORITIES

1. Retain and strengthen federal affirmative-action programs
2. Balance the budget as soon as possible
3. Strengthen education funding
4. Expand job training and tax incentives for job creation
5. Repeal NAFTA

PLEASING CROWDS IS NOT ENOUGH

NAME: Alan Lee Keyes
BORN: August 7, 1950
EDUCATION: B.A. and M.A., Harvard University
OCCUPATION: Radio talk show host
FAMILY: Married to Jocelyn Keyes; three children
QUOTE: "Abortion is a moral wrong. We have the opportunity, the duty, to stand up and say, 'Nay.'"

PERHAPS THE LOUDEST AND MOST INSISTENT VOICE among the pack of Republican candidates is that of Alan Lee Keyes, a forty-four-year-old, Harvard-educated radio talk show host who revels in being more confrontationally conservative than either Pat Buchanan or Robert Dornan. That Keyes is African-American makes his comparison of government-funded abortions as "a kind of slavery of black Americans" all the more provocative.

But Keyes loves to provoke, and he has been wowing Republican audiences across the country, eclipsing other rightists such as Buchanan and Dornan and stealing the show from pack leaders Dole and Gramm. The news media do not know how to deal with a black ultraconservative who is articulate, blunt, and unabashed by his radicalism, so he largely has been treated as a kind of novelty act that cheers up GOP activists but does not actually bear on the election campaign itself.

That view is not accurate, however. When the *Washington Post* prominently displayed the results of a straw poll of Virginia Republicans, reporting that Pat Buchanan had trounced Dole and Gramm, who had run a distant third and fourth, respectively, not mentioned in the article was the fact that Keyes had run Buchanan a close second. At a 1995 GOP summer rally in Phoenix, which was supposed to be a love fest for Gramm backers, Keyes's fiery stem-winder of a speech stressed morality as a campaign goal and attacked the Democrats for offering "a dingy material prosperity that forsakes faith, family, and country." He won standing ovations in Phoenix and then repeated the performance at another supposed demonstration of Gramm's drawing power in South Carolina. Competitor Dornan, who also went to South Carolina, reported ruefully, "I got two standing ovations in South Carolina; Keyes got four."

But can Keyes get the votes? Probably not enough. Keyes can boast tours at the U.S. State Department during the Reagan administration, including a stint as ambassador to UNESCO; he also was assistant secretary of state for international-organization affairs. He has not done well as a candidate for governor twice in his home state of Maryland, in part because of his unwillingness to ask for help from the state's GOP establishment. To be sure, that is part of his attraction to Republicans who are in a rebellious mood. Alan Keyes is his own man, even if no one votes for him.

PRIORITIES

1. Enact tough federal anti-abortion laws
2. End affirmative-action programs
3. Implement tougher anti-crime measures and mandatory sentencing laws
4. Require the death penalty for drug dealers
5. Take an internationalist approach to foreign policy

THINKING THIRD PARTY

NAME: Lowell P. Weicker, Jr.
BORN: May 16, 1931
EDUCATION: B.A., Harvard University; LL.B., University
    of Virginia
OCCUPATION: Consultant
FAMILY: Married to Claudia Weicker (third marriage);
    seven children
QUOTE: "Lick the problem and get on with life."

WHERE LOWELL WEICKER DIFFERS FROM OTHER BACK-
of-the-pack candidates is that he is firmly convinced that if
he runs as an independent candidate this summer, he could
actually win the race.

For one thing, he would have to raise less money. "The
regular parties will have to spend much more. An independent's major campaign expense is getting access to the ballot in all fifty states, and that is largely petition-gathering
and some television. A rough ballpark guess for that would
be $30 million for a first-class job, and that money can be
raised by the right independent."

Weicker has certainly learned to be an independent. He
started his political career as a Republican state legislator,
congressman, and senator, but was always an annoyance to
GOP leaders, who insisted on discipline within the rank

and file. He used his seat on the Senate Watergate Committee to hector the Nixon administration; finally, after he denounced the Reagan administration's invasion of Grenada and attack on Libya, Connecticut Republicans denied him his fourth term in the 1988 elections.

Two years later Weicker was swept into the governor's mansion as head of the Connecticut Party and promptly enraged his supporters by pushing through the state's first income tax—although the rage abated somewhat when the crippling budget deficit was erased. Now, two years into a career as a consultant, Weicker is hammering away at what he calls "the last remaining monolith since the fall of Communism: the U.S. two-party system."

"The question that faces me is that I am having more fun than I have had in thirty-two years, I have more time with my kids, and so do I really want to give up a year of my life to talk about what I think the important choices are?" Weicker said recently.

"The question after that is who do I hurt, or help, if I do run. Because I sure do not want to help anything I see coming off the Republican bench this season. I would have helped the old Bob Dole, but this Bob Dole is chasing down that hard right in the party; forget it. Maybe if [it were Massachusetts governor] Bill Weld, I would have to think.

"Clinton is something else. I am a lot closer in belief to the President, and I believe he is a decent man. But there is a question of leadership there that I can't ignore," he adds. "But in the end I have to come back to the fact that both parties and their probable standard-bearers *are* the problem that threatens this country."

As with the GOP nomination hopefuls, who play fractional counting games as they calculate their chances in this primary or that caucus, Weicker would need to depend on his ability to accumulate enough middle-to-moderately-left support from disaffected Republicans and disenchanted Democrats to make him a player.

"You probably will have two independent candidates in addition to the party nominees. I am assuming that Ross Perot is in the race. But none of them has enough of an intellectual appeal on the issues," he explains.

Like nearly every other candidate, Weicker has just published a book about his background and beliefs, *Maverick: A Life in Politics,* in which he argues that his experience as an independent governor who cut spending and balanced the budget would serve well in Washington.

What Weicker offers as President is pretty much along the lines of the new Democrat philosophy of pragmatic liberalism: government that works and is fair, nonintrusive, and less threatening to citizens. This is an agenda that Bill Clinton espoused in 1992 and then abandoned. Weicker's commitment to working with handicapped children through the Special Olympics, his efforts to restructure the mental-health facilities of Connecticut, and a general fiscal conservatism on budgets and taxes, he believes, are a mix that will attract enough reasoning voters of both parties for him to win the White House.

Is that group large enough? Weicker cites recent opinion polls that argue yes.

"If you could capture in time right now the American people and throw them into a voting booth, the Republicans and Democrats are going out the window. I have contacts with the polling groups of both major parties and what I get is that the Republicans, yes, are on the radar screen all right. The Democrats aren't even on the radar screen; they don't compute. But mention *independent*, and the [expletive] thing goes through the roof. That's the hard-nosed poling truth of it. And with that mood in place, I can win. Or someone like me."

<u>PRIORITIES</u>

1. Enact tough budget controls and spending limits
2. Cut the federal deficit
3. Reestablish diplomatic relations with Cuba
4. Implement tax cuts for the middle class
5. Extend NAFTA to other Latin American nations
6. Expand federal treatment programs for AIDS

TABLES

1996 PRIMARY CALENDAR

DATE	STATE	CONTEST	DEM. DELEGATES	REP. DELEGATES	ELECTORAL VOTES
Feb. 6	Louisiana	Caucus (R)	—	21	9
Feb. 12	Iowa	Caucus	56	25	7
Feb. 20	New Hampshire	Primary	26	16	4
Feb. 24	Delaware	Primary	21	12	3
Feb. 27	Arizona	Primary (R)	—	39	8
	North Dakota	Primary (R)	—	18	3
	South Dakota	Primary (R)	—	18	3
Mar. 2	South Carolina	Primary (R)	—	37	8
Mar. 5	Colorado	Primary	58	27	8
	Georgia	Primary	91	42	13
	Idaho	Caucus (D)	24	—	2
	Maryland	Primary	85	32	10
	Massachusetts	Primary	114	37	10
	Minnesota	Caucus (D)	92	—	12
	Vermont	Primary (R)	—	12	3
	Washington	Caucus (D)	91	—	9

1996 PRIMARY CALENDAR (CONT.)

DATE	STATE	CONTEST	DEM. DELEGATES	REP. DELEGATES	ELECTORAL VOTES
Mar. 7	Missouri	Caucus (D)	93	35	11
	New York	Primary	298	102	33
	North Dakota	Caucus (D)	22	—	3
Mar. 9	Arizona	Caucus (D)	52	—	3
	South Carolina	Primary (D)	52	8	8
Mar. 10	Nevada	Caucus (D)	27	14	4
Mar. 12	Florida	Primary	177	98	25
	Hawaii	Caucus (D)	30	14	4
	Maine	Primary	32	15	4
	Mississippi	Primary	29	32	7
	Oklahoma	Primary	53	38	8
	Rhode Island	Primary	31	16	4
	Tennessee	Primary	83	37	11
Mar. 19	Illinois	Primary	194	69	22
	Michigan	Primary	158	57	13
	Ohio	Primary	171	67	21

1996 PRIMARY CALENDAR (CONT.)

DATE	STATE	CONTEST	DEM. DELEGATES	REP. DELEGATES	ELECTORAL VOTES
Mar. 19	Wisconsin	Primary	93	36	11
Mar. 23	Wyoming	Caucus (D)	19	20	1
Mar. 25	Utah	Caucus (D)	30	28	5
Mar. 26	California	Primary	423	163	54
	Connecticut	Primary	55	27	8
	Vermont	Caucus (D)	22	—	9
Apr. 2	Kansas	Primary	41	31	6
	Minnesota	Primary (R)	—	33	10
Apr. 4	Alaska	Caucus (D)	19	19	3
Apr. 13	Virginia	Caucus (D)	96	53	13
Apr. 23	Pennsylvania	Primary	195	73	23
May 7	Indiana	Primary	89	52	10
	North Carolina	Primary	98	58	12
May 14	Nebraska	Primary	33	24	3
	West Virginia	Primary	42	18	3
May 21	Arkansas	Primary	48	20	4

1996 PRIMARY CALENDAR (CONT.)

DATE	STATE	CONTEST	DEM. DELEGATES	REP. DELEGATES	ELECTORAL VOTES
May 21	Oregon	Primary	56	23	5
May 28	Idaho	Primary (R)	—	23	2
	Kentucky	Primary	61	26	5
	Washington	Primary (R)	—	36	9
June 4	Alabama	Primary	66	39	7
	Montana	Primary	25	14	1
	New Jersey	Primary	120	48	13
	New Mexico	Primary	34	14	3
Unsched-uled	District of Columbia	Primary	—	—	3

Note: A dash indicates that the number of delegates has not yet been determined.

(Source: Federal Elections Commission)

PAST NOVEMBER ELECTION RESULTS

1992 PRESIDENTIAL ELECTION

	NUMBER OF VOTES	% OF VOTE	ELECTORAL VOTES
Bill Clinton	44,908,254	43	370
George Bush	39,242,243	37	426
H. Ross Perot	19,741,055	19	–

1988 PRESIDENTIAL ELECTION

	NUMBER OF VOTES	% OF VOTE	ELECTORAL VOTES
George Bush	48,881,221	53	426
Michael Dukakis	41,805,122	46	111

1984 PRESIDENTIAL ELECTION

	NUMBER OF VOTES	% OF VOTE	ELECTORAL VOTES
Ronald Reagan	54,281,858	59	525
Walter F. Mondale	37,457,215	41	13

1980 PRESIDENTIAL ELECTION

	NUMBER OF VOTES	% OF VOTE	ELECTORAL VOTES
Ronald Reagan	43,899,248	49.8	489
Jimmy Carter	38,481,435	43.6	49
John B. Anderson	5,719,437	6.5	–

(Source: Federal Elections Commission)

HOW THE STATES STACK UP FOR THE DEMOCRATS AND REPUBLICANS
BASED ON ELECTION PATTERNS SINCE 1980

FIRM for Democrats
District of Columbia, Hawaii, Maryland, Massachusetts, Virginia, West Virginia
Electoral Votes: 34

FIRM for Republicans
Alabama, Arizona, Idaho, Indiana, Kansas, Mississippi, Montana, Nebraska, New Hampshire, New Mexico, North Carolina, North Dakota, Ohio, Oklahoma, South Carolina, South Dakota, Texas, Utah, Vermont, Virginia, Wyoming
Electoral Votes: 170

LEANING for Democrats
Arkansas, Illinois, New York, Oregon, Rhode Island, Washington
Electoral Votes: 83

LEANING for Republicans
Alaska, Florida, Iowa, Kentucky, Maine, Missouri
Electoral Votes: 58

UP FOR GRABS
California, Colorado, Delaware, Georgia, Louisiana, Michigan, Minnesota, Nevada, New Jersey, Pennsylvania, Tennessee, Wisconsin
Electoral Votes: 198

FORECAST: The winner must carry California, Pennsylvania, and Michigan plus *all* the states in his party's base.

(Source: Federal Elections Commission)

U.S. SENATE SEATS UP FOR REELECTION
IN 1996

INCUMBENT	STATE	FIRST ELECTED	COMMENTS
Max Baucus (D)	Montana	1978	
Bill Bradley (D)	New Jersey	1973	Not running
Hank Brown (R)	Colorado	1991	Not running
Thad Cochran (R)	Mississippi	1978	
William Cohen (R)	Maine	1979	
Larry Craig (R)	Idaho	1991	
Pete Domenici (R)	New Mexico	1973	
James Exon (D)	Nebraska	1979	Not running
Phil Gramm (R)	Texas	1985	Can run for presidency and Senate
Tom Harkin (D)	Iowa	1985	
Mark Hatfield (R)	Oregon	1967	
Howell Heflin (D)	Alabama	1979	Not running
Jesse Helms (R)	North Carolina	1973	
James Inhofe (R)	Oklahoma	1994	Two-year term
J. Bennett Johnston (D)	Louisiana	1972	Not running
Nancy Kassebaum (R)	Kansas	1978	
John Kerry (D)	Massachusetts	1985	
Carl Levin (D)	Michigan	1979	
Mitch McConnell (R)	Kentucky	1985	
Sam Nunn (D)	Georgia	1972	Not running
Claiborne Pell (D)	Rhode Island	1961	Not running
John D. Rockefeller (D)	West Virginia	1985	
Paul Simon (D)	Illinois	1985	Not running
Alan Simpson (R)	Wyoming	1979	
Robert Smith (R)	New Hampshire	1990	
Ted Stevens (R)	Alaska	1968	

INCUMBENT	STATE	FIRST ELECTED	COMMENTS
Fred Thompson (R)	Tennessee	1994	Two-year term
Strom Thurmond (R)	South Carolina	1956	
John Warner (R)	Virginia	1979	
Paul Wellstone (D)	Minnesota	1991	

James Srodes is a twenty-eight-year veteran of Washington journalism. He has been *Financial World* magazine's bureau chief since 1985. He also writes a weekly column for the *Sunday Telegraph* of London. He has covered Capitol Hill and the White House for United Press International, *Business Week,* and *Forbes*.

Srodes is the coauthor of investigative business biographies of John Z. DeLorean and Ivan Boesky. His biography of former CIA director Allen W. Dulles will be published later in 1996. He and his wife, Cecile, an attorney, live in Washington, D.C.

Financial World magazine contributing editor **Arthur Jones** is the Washington, D.C.–based editor-at-large of the independent newsweekly *The National Catholic Reporter*. He is a former New York associate editor and European bureau chief of *Forbes* magazine and a former *Financial Times of London* correspondent who writes also for *World Trade* magazine.

Other books by British-born, Oxford-educated Jones, a U.S. citizen, include *The Decline of Capital, Malcolm Forbes: Peripatetic Millionaire,* and *Reassessing*. He and his wife, Margie, have three grown children and one grandchild, Tyler.